Price Dept.

$90 — McNally
$75 — Cahill
#135 — KENT
#30 — Mom Dixie

#9 — LOAN
#7 —
———————
#16 → Bodie

THERE <u>IS</u> A BETTER WAY TO SELL

THERE <u>IS</u>
A BETTER WAY
TO SELL

SIDNEY EDLUND

amacom

A DIVISION OF AMERICAN MANAGEMENT ASSOCIATION

International standard book number: 0-8144-5312-0
Library of Congress catalog card number: 72-84117

First printing

Foreword

As a 15-year associate of Sidney Edlund and as a collaborator on this book and on scores of his other marketing and management projects, I know something about the man and the book.

In *There IS a Better Way to Sell* he turns a penetrating mind upon the major problem of every salesman: how to make substantial sales gains on a continuing basis. Early in the book he presents the central core of his well-proven sales-training methods: the need to establish those habits essential to top productivity. Then he presents, step by step, the tested techniques that enable every salesman to meet that need.

One basic philosophy marks Sidney Edlund's entire career. When challenged with a problem, he plugs away until he finds a better-than-existing solution. This "there must be a better way" approach explains why he joined Wm. A. Rogers without title and became General Sales Manager, why he moved on to Pine Bros. without title and became President, and why he repeated this process at Life Savers, Inc.

As Senior Partner of Sidney Edlund Associates, Marketing Consultants, he has personally served over 200 clients. These include small corporations and 18 listed on the Big Board; numerous banks, insurance companies, and trade associations; and over a score of consulting firms that have sought his help in marketing their services.

Recognizing that visual presentation is a powerful but often badly misused selling tool, he organized the National Visual Presentation Association (now the National Visual Communication Association). His *Your Visual Presentation—And How to Use It* has served as an effective guide to over 75,000 salesmen.

Also, he organized and for 19 years directed the famous Man Marketing Clinics, now under the auspices of the Sales Executives Club of New York. These free clinics have helped over half a million individuals to make their most difficult sale: selling themselves. Which tells you that he is a very human being. Out of these experiences he wrote (with his wife Mary) *Pick Your Job and Land It!*, which was condensed in *Reader's Digest*.

Sidney Edlund has tested the concepts presented in this book in his down-to-earth way. He has tried them out in the field with over 1,000 salesmen with sales ranging from six-figure capital equipment contracts, and has tried them out while tapping on doors to sell *The Book of Knowledge*. He has successfully applied these concepts in scores of organizations and has trained others to do likewise. His *Selling More Lumber . . . Profitably* has been called the "bible for selling lumber." Similar praise has been accorded his *7 Keys to Better Wholesaling* and his *More Business for Your Bank,* which has helped many an officer to sell more creatively. He has exposed his ideas freely from the platforms of sales executives clubs, in American Management Association seminars, and at corporate and trade association gatherings. Small wonder, then, that in *There IS a Better Way to Sell* he makes his case vividly and with justifiable conviction—and always with the problems of the salesman very much in mind.

ARTHUR MITCHELL

Contents

1

Habit Formation:
The Better Way to Sell

Ours is a consumer-oriented society. People want more and more of the good things of life. Industry is geared to supply them. All of which means bigger opportunities for making sales. But the real point is: Do salesmen take sufficient advantage of these opportunities?

They should, because more than any other workers salesmen write their own pay checks. Nevertheless, the evidence is clear that they fall far short of their potential. An intensive three-year study by the Sales Manpower Division of the Sales Executives Club of New York underscores this situation. The report shows that the crushing cost of selling is due essentially to low productivity, to the disturbing turnover rate, and to inadequate training.

On the surface, many salesmen and many sales organizations have risen to the challenge posed by the Sales Manpower Division's findings. Witness the more than 3,000 texts on selling which have been avidly read by salesmen, the business school courses, the regularly scheduled sales meetings, and company sales-training programs. Obviously, almost all salesmen have been exposed to the fundamentals of selling. And they are well aware of the relationship between their sales and their earnings.

While salesmen and their companies have profited appreciably from the numerous educational activities noted above, the results have hardly been commensurate with the effort. Far too little of that effort has been translated into consistent action. Not, mind you, for lack of practical content. When a salesman reads a text or participates in a sales-training program, he usually comes away with a number of ideas which he knows will enable him to be more productive. But most of them fade from his mind before he adopts them.

Why? Because one essential ingredient has usually been missing: a definite technique for the development of *habit-forming* applications. This is true for every area of selling, as my own and numerous other studies have confirmed.

MOTIVATION

Every salesman agrees that the more strongly he is motivated, the more productive he becomes. But how many can unhesitatingly identify the strongest of all self-motivating forces—the motivation that comes from having meaningful goals? And how many actually apply this powerful stimulator to their own best advantage?

Only a few. Yet the widespread and *habitual* application of this most effective of all self-motivating forces would help each man increase the number of constructive calls—and thus boost his ratio of sales to calls.

PRINCIPLES OF SELLING

"Do most salesmen apply the basic principles of communication and selling consistently? Raise your hand if you agree."

Whether I pose that question to groups of salesmen or to sales managers from the platforms of sales executives clubs around the country, only an occasional hand goes up.

But then I ask: "When salesmen learn to apply basic principles consciously and consistently, do they sell considerably more goods and services?" This time every hand shoots up.

Clearly, the route to more sales and bigger earnings rests not only on basic principles but also on ways of building habits of application.

CREATIVE SELLING

Every salesman knows that he will sell more goods and services when he sells creatively—that is, when he gets close to the prospect's problems and helps to solve them. Yet how many salesmen consistently apply the techniques of creative selling? Only a small minority, as various surveys have reported.

Again, the 3,000 texts on selling may provide much of the know-how, but the habit-building follow-through has been neglected.

SELLING TOOLS

"Right now, where can you find a big percentage of visual presentations and other tools designed to help salesmen increase their sales?"

Salesmen will tell you that they are in their cars or

homes, gathering dust. And all too often when salesmen do use them, their prospects wish they had been left behind.

Yet when visual presentations are properly designed and employed, their habitual use has enabled entire sales forces to register dramatic increases in sales volume.

BUILDING ESSENTIAL HABITS

Developed out of rich firing-line experience, *There IS a Better Way to Sell* includes a number of new twists and techniques. But the book revolves essentially around those fundamentals which the more astute salesmen and sales managers have long practiced. For the problem is not what to do but how to apply known principles consistently and more effectively. Solving this problem is the real purpose of this book. Designed as a self-training program, it provides an exceedingly simple method for any salesman to develop the most productive selling habits and procedures.

All he needs to do is to concentrate on one major point at a time, long enough to establish the essential habits of application; only then should he go on to the next point. Yet as simple and effective as this method is, it is seldom practiced.

This explains why the great majority of salesmen fail year after year to make greater use of the fundamentals of their profession, and why their sales and earnings remain far below their potential.

There are just seven ways in which practically any salesman can increase his productivity and earnings year after year. These practices define the scope of this book. Thus as you follow the step-by-step procedures outlined in the following chapters—with every point illustrated by real-life examples—you will gradually build the habits that will help you consistently to

Motivate yourself to greater achievement.

Apply *basic principles* of communication and selling consciously and more effectively.

Do more *creative selling.*

Make better use of *selling tools.*

Improve your approaches to frequently *recurring situations.*

Manage time to greater advantage.

Sell yourself more effectively to gain rapport with customers and prospects.

Note how tightly these fundamentals hang together. You can hardly apply basic principles more consistently unless you first motivate yourself to greater effort. Nor can you develop more creative approaches without learning to apply the principles of communication and selling more effectively.

Because of these interlocking relationships, the text builds up a powerful impact as you progress from one point to the next. That is, every improvement in one area immediately affects performance in another. Thus from the very first chapter your sales and earnings will begin to register improvement.

To make the most of this book you must read it *actively.* One good way is to first read it quickly to glimpse its underlying principles and to get the feel of it. Then go back and read each chapter thoughtfully. Focus on those things closest to your own problems. Underline points of importance to you. Or use a pencil and notebook. Add your own habit-building ideas to those suggested at the end of the chapter. Concentrate on applying the fundamentals presented until you do so habitually. Then, and only then, move on and do the same with the next chapter.

Because you practice this application on your daily

rounds, you establish each precious selling habit *without cutting one minute into your selling time.* And because the learning process is mostly a matter of concentrated doing, nearly every improvement in selling methods occurs during the application phase. What counts most is not how thoroughly you read this book but how consistently you follow through.

Every phase of this sales-building program has been thoroughly proved in practice by salesmen for large firms and small, for industrial, consumer, and service organizations. Evidence appears in every chapter: actual examples of spiraling sales and increasing earnings. With consistent follow-through, the habit-forming methods of *There IS a Better Way to Sell* will help experienced men and trainees to achieve greater sales volume and greater job satisfaction.

Use it consistently and write bigger and bigger pay checks for yourself, year after year.

Applying Basic Principles

H. P. Snow, former president of the Detroit Twist Drill Company, tells a significant story: "When we started building our sales organization, we proceeded on the theory that the selling of drills called for highly technical knowledge. When we needed salesmen, we took experts out of our manufacturing departments and put them to work selling goods instead of making them. But with some exceptions they did not succeed on the selling end.

"We could not understand at first where they fell down. All the logic of the situation demanded that a technical product of this kind, to be used by experts, should also be sold by experts.

"Sweeping aside theory and considering the cold facts, we determined that selling ability comes first. We learned that selling is selling—no matter what the object sold—*and that to sell more twist drills is mainly to adapt fundamental principles that apply in selling any article of merchandise.*"

Practically all salesmen have been exposed to sound selling principles through sales meetings, training sessions, and books. What's more, they accept them gratefully; they know that they contain the essence of successful salesmanship.

Yet of the scores of sales managers and hundreds of salesmen I've queried almost all agree that few salesmen make consistent use of these major principles, which they realize would insure more and bigger sales and higher earnings.

Why don't they? In four words: "Too much, too fast."

They do not gain a *working* knowledge of the principles because they're deluged with far more than they can meaningfully absorb. One training manual speaks of "120 ways to more sales" and "80 ways of overcoming objections." Thrust so much at a man in one dose and it just won't sink in: the ideas do not become a part of his everyday thinking, actions, and language. Even less can he establish the precious habits of application which insure selling success.

Do it the Ben Franklin way: one step at a time

You learn by doing, by practice. And you make that doing habitual when you practice just one new skill or principle at a time.

Canny Ben Franklin worked that out a long time ago. As a young man Franklin set out to lead a life of "moral virtue." He read everything he could find on the subject, then drew up a list of 13 basic "virtues": justice, industry, frugality, humility, and the like.

Fired with enthusiasm, he plunged headlong into the practice of all 13 virtues at one time. At the end of each day he put a black mark against the virtues he had offended that day.

For all his determination and will power, he was unable to go through one day without violating some of those virtues. Studying the problem, young Ben hit upon a new approach. He decided to concentrate on one virtue at a time.

For example, he would go day after day applying the virtue of industry until it became a fixed habit and the black marks disappeared for good. *Only then would he turn to the practice of the next.*

Following this method, he trained himself to the point that he could go day after day without one black mark. But he became so proud of what he had done that he set a black mark against humility!

Ben Franklin applied this formula to everything he had to learn throughout his life. Together with his own innate ability, it helped him become in turn master printer, salesman, inventor, statesman, and diplomat.

THE SEVEN BASIC PRINCIPLES OF SELLING

It worked for Ben Franklin. And it has worked for everyone I've ever known who followed his example. That's why after long study and experience in training thousands of salesmen, I evolved a way of adapting Franklin's build-a-habit technique to the principles of selling. This simple three-step formula underlies every aspect of *There IS a Better Way to Sell:*

1. Take a small number of the most basic and powerful selling principles, the seven that make for more and better sales.
2. Concentrate on one principle at a time. Apply and practice it until its use becomes habitual.
3. Then move on to the next.

Not one of these principles is new. Their power derives from conscious recognition backed by consistent application. Here they are:

1. *Objectives:* the key to direction
2. *Preparation:* the key to more productive presentations
3. *Inquiry:* the key to your prospect's interests
4. *Benefits:* the key to buying decisions
5. *wRap-up:* the key to winning acceptance step-by-step
6. *Objections:* the key to meeting resistance
7. *Closing:* the key to more and bigger orders

The initial letters of these seven principles form the catchword O PIB'ROC, which I have coined for easy recall.

When I was president of Kelvinator National Salesmen's Institute, we had our salesmen send us reports of the sales they felt they would not have made had they not applied one or more of the principles and techniques incorporated in O PIB'ROC. In the very first year we received over 10,000 reports of such sales, ranging from $200 to substantial sums.

Let me repeat. These salesmen reported that they would not have made those 10,000 sales if they had not learned to apply the O PIB'ROC principles—an ability which any salesman can acquire.

There's an added beauty to this. In learning to apply the O PIB'ROC formula, you suffer no loss of selling time. Experience has shown that it takes about a month of concentrated application to start establishing each habit. And because the principles are equally valid for all purposeful communication, you can work on building these valuable habits when you are relaxing at home or at the club, writing a letter, or talking on the phone, as well as when you are selling in the field.

These O PIB'ROC principles are so potent that intensive use of any one of them will reflect itself in a rising sales curve. Apply all of them as they should be used and your earnings will grow at an even faster pace.

Remember: reading through this book will give you a general view of the seven ways to bigger sales and earnings. But only when you go back and start concentrating on each factor for your habit-building month will this reading start to pay real dividends.

2

How to Motivate Yourself

Why does one man make it where another man fails? Osborne Elliott, chief executive officer of Newsweek, Inc., addressed himself to that question as he contemplated the careers of the chief executives of some of the country's largest corporations for his book *Men at the Top*.

On the surface, the men he was studying had little in common. One had won his college degree with honors; another had been a campus playboy; a third had dropped out of school when a good selling job had come his way. In temperament, they ranged the spectrum from outgoing geniality to self-centered intensity. And all had reached the top in different ways.

In sum, each was an individual sharply differentiated from any of the others. What quality did they share to explain their mutual success?

The more Elliott researched and pondered, the clearer the answer became. Even in their early years, he found,

12   *There IS a Better Way to Sell*

most men at the top knew exactly what they wanted. They always had an eye on the top rung of their personal career ladders and headed toward it consciously. Without exception, they all attributed the dedication that marked their careers to their clearly held goals. Everything they did was colored by this long-range vision. And every step along the way merely whetted their desire to reach the top—as all eventually did.

TAPPING YOUR INTERNAL RESOURCES

Why do objectives generate so much power? Because the pull of a worthy goal awakens your reserve powers: those hidden assets that everyone has but few draw upon sufficiently.

William James, America's great psychologist, made no bones about it. "Compared to what we ought to be," he wrote, "we are only half awake. The human individual possesses physical and mental resources which he habitually fails to use."

Tapping those inner resources more fully is the key to success in any endeavor. In his classic *The Origin of Species* Charles Darwin underlined the point: "Men differ less in their abilities than in the degree to which they use them."

In short, what sets the superlative off from the mediocre is not how much you have but how much you use. And that in turn rests upon the strength of your inner drive. As "Whitey" Ford once put it in an article on the ingredients of major league success: "First you've got to have desire."

Not that "can do" factors may safely be neglected. It is

just that "will do" factors are somewhat more important because they bring into play more of those hidden resources which help the motivated man surpass himself. And of all the motivational forces which tug at our dormant powers no other even approaches the powerful impact of a man's own meaningful goals.

wryly - RT - twisted distorted.

How Sam Bassett did it

Let me illustrate the point.

Several years ago I was flying to a sales meeting with several executives from a company which sold fruits and syrups to the fountain trade. Jim Grant, the president, remarked wryly: "There's one chap who will be there whom we should have fired."

"Why?" I asked.

"He's just not producing. We're giving him a little more time only because he hasn't been with us too long."

Believing firmly that any salesman can do a much better job if he has clearly defined goals to shoot for, I suggested that I coach this man.

The president shrugged. "Go ahead, Sid, if you like. But you'll be wasting your time. I don't think that Sam Bassett will ever be a salesman."

I spent as much time with Bassett as I could. Here's what we talked about over the three-day period:

"Sam, what do you hope to be doing 15 years from now?"

"I'd like to be a sales manager."

"In what field?"

"The one I'm in [fruits and syrups]."

"Why this one?"

Shrugge — to draw up (the shoulders), as in doubt, indifference etc.

"Because a man with merchandising ideas can go places in it. Besides, I like the people I meet and the situations I face."

"That's fine. You know what you want and why. The trouble is, you haven't been using your capacity in this direction. So tell me, how do you now propose to achieve your goal?"

"I expect to plug at it."

"That seems somewhat vague. Could you be more specific?"

"Can you suggest how?"

"Let me pose a question. In the next 15 years do you think you could learn more than anyone else about what it takes to move fruits and syrups from the back of the fountains to the customers?"

After deep thought, he said: "That's a tall order."

"Maybe it is, but do you think it is possible?"

"I might not go all the way, but many a thing becomes possible when you make up your mind to it."

"Would it change your life any?"

"It sure would."

"In what way?"

"I'd do many things differently. For one, I'd have to work behind the counter on weekends until I got a better understanding of selling syrups from the dealer's angle."

"Would that be agreeable to your family?"

"If I did it in moderation in order to improve myself, I think they'd be pleased."

"What else would be different?"

"I'd examine menus in my calls. If one featured peach melba, for instance, I'd find out how much business it produced.

"When I came across a lime rickey window, I'd want to know how many rickeys the dealer averaged before the display, how many during the promotion, and whether it developed extra business or helped sales of sandwiches and other store items. On my next trip I'd check to see if the promotion had any lasting effect."

"Sam," I said, "your plan is really shaping up."

He continued: "I'd have to read trade papers more thoughtfully, clip worthwhile formulas and other ideas for merchandising syrups, and put them in a scrapbook. I'd have to ask questions of many dealers—talk to them about their selling problems and promotional efforts—and get records of results. Why," he exclaimed, "before too long, I'd have a regular encyclopedia on the subject."

"You certainly would," I replied, "and you should keep it well indexed. Then, if you tucked it under your arm and used it whenever you had an opportunity to talk with dealers about merchandising fruits and syrups, do you think it might turn out to be the most important book in the industry?"

"I don't know about the book. But one thing is sure. I'd be making a lot more sales."

"Do you think it would be fun?"

"It sure would!"

Three months later Jim Grant, the president of the firm, phoned me. "Sid," he boomed, "what did you do with that man Bassett down in Florida?"

"Why do you ask?"

"He caught fire right after the meeting and he's been doing more business every week. Actually in relation to his calls, his orders have increased about 25 percent since our meeting. What's more, he has pushed up the average number of items on each order from three to over seven.

"But there's more to it than that. His reports, his correspondence, his comments—all show that he is a completely different person!"

And Sam *was* a different person. Or at least a newly awakened one. For now he had worthy objectives—*a fundamental for tapping his valuable inner resources.*

THE VERDICT OF RESEARCH

Going beyond individual experiences, such highly regarded psychologists as Saul Gellerman, Abraham Maslow, and Frederick Herzberg have confirmed the self-motivating power of objectives over years of intensive research.

"The most common bias is the underestimate of what the individual is capable of achieving," writes Gellerman in his *Management by Motivation.* "As a result, relatively few people make a sustained effort to reach the limit of their potentialities. To assume a group of people is inherently incapable of exceeding a certain level of attainment is the easy, and regrettably common, consolation of a small mind."

The individual attains these limits, Maslow points out, by the pull of what he calls self-actualization needs, "which include the pursuit of personal goals as well as planning, executing, and getting results." It is this pursuit which impels a man to reach inside himself for those hidden assets that spell the difference between realizing his potential and falling short of it.

"No wind is the right wind"

For all the evidence to the contrary, someone will always say: "Maybe objectives will shake a man up. But in the last analysis we all know it's the breaks that count."

Breaks do play a part. But some people capitalize on them, others do not. Indeed, a man without a goal may not recognize a break even when it stares him in the face.

The Roman philosopher Seneca summed it up neatly 2,000 years ago. "When you have no port of call," he wrote, "no wind is the right wind."

Conversely, the effect of worthy goals and plans can be somewhat uncanny. When you work out for yourself where you want to be five or ten years from now and just what you will do about that goal this year, this month, and this day, you become a different and more dynamic person. Your thinking changes and so do your actions. Friends, customers, management—all those you contact regularly—become aware of it. Much that we attribute to luck can be so explained.

Was it luck...

One wholesale lumber representative tells an illuminating story. "Last fall," he says, "a customer asked me how he could keep his help busy during the slack winter months. It so happened that I had some literature on building picnic tables out of redwood, different kinds of redwood fence panels, and redwood cattle feed bunks. I discussed the possibilities with the dealer and left him the material.

"Not long after the call a snowstorm slowed up building for more than six weeks. My idea kept the dealer's men busy all through that time. More to the point, he sold everything they built. Now he's planning an even bigger specialty building program this winter. This idea boosted my redwood sales and put me in solid with my customer."

... or the motivating power of his objectives?

This representative told the story at a sales-training workshop as an example of the power of objectives. "But having the answer to the dealer's problem right on you was just a matter of luck," some of his fellow salesmen objected.

"True," the representative conceded. "Still, the incident occurred not long after I set myself a goal of making more constructive calls. That's why I was primed to take advantage of any such situation. Having literature available was part of my plan. And if I hadn't had the answer with me, you can bet I'd have looked into it and found an idea for my next call."

SEVEN STEPS TO GREATER SELF-MOTIVATION

There's no question about it: motivation comes almost entirely from within. Indeed, I have never seen it fail. Always, the single step of working out ambitious growth objectives inspires a perceptible increase in sales. How you do it will become clear as you consider each of the seven steps to greater self-motivation:

1. Set your own objectives.
2. Make your goals measurable.
3. Aim high: put "stretch" in your goals.
4. Add essential corollary objectives.
5. Share your objectives.
6. Plan to achieve your goals.
7. Live your objectives.

SET YOUR OWN OBJECTIVES

In the past five years I have met with over a thousand sales managers at various American Management Association meetings. "How many of you," I have asked, "rather than assigning management-established quotas to your men, have asked them to develop their own bold territorial objectives—in keeping, of course, with the broad overall objectives of management?"

Only a minority, I have found, follow this procedure. Yet practically all who do swear by this practice.

Why? Simply because their men bring in more business that way. As one executive put it: "A man runs hardest after his own goals."

He put it to the test

The general sales manager of a leading life insurance company tells an interesting story in this connection. Having been impressed by a seminar on management by objectives, he decided to test the effect of goal setting at the individual level. To this end, he picked two sample territories that were fairly well matched in the abilities of their field managers and the productivity of their salesmen.

Company sales objectives were outlined in detail for the four field managers involved. But from there on matters diverged.

"Can you and your men together work out goals you will shoot for individually, within the framework of the company's objectives?" the sales manager asked the two "Group One" managers. After meeting with their crews, the two field supervisors reported the goals their men had selected. Five things were included:

Managing time more fruitfully.
Cultivating 50 percent more prospects than were currently on their lists.
Selling a more rounded line.
Learning more about favorable applications.
Increasing sales volume by 40 percent over the previous year.

At this point the top sales executive issued a directive to the "Group Two" managers and salesmen, saddling them with the same goals Group One had freely chosen. A week later, after Group One asked if management would provide some training sessions on applications, Group Two was told that a training course had been scheduled which all must attend.

Six months later a progress review disclosed some startling divergences between the two groups. Both had increased their output. But whereas Group One was running some 10 percent above its self-chosen goals, Group Two was about 20 percent below its imposed quotas.

"When we explained it was all an experiment," the general sales manager reported, "we got at the morale factors. Group Two supervisors and men felt they were being 'pushed around.' The Group One people were challenged by their own goals."

Group Two salesmen resented the training sessions because "no one discussed it with us beforehand." Group One welcomed them "as an aid to achieving our objectives."

Winding up the story, the sales manager remarked: "We have since spread the idea of self-chosen goals—goals set by those responsible for achieving them—to our entire sales force. In every case work and morale have improved."

"I can do better than you Yankees"

I saw this powerful psychological force operate for the first time with a consulting client a number of years ago. The firm manufactures a specialty line sold in drug, variety, and news stores. Nine experienced salesmen cover the country, selling to wholesalers and chain outlets. At the annual sales meeting in December the men are assigned

@mid — a mid *Among in the*
Middle of.

their quotas for the coming year. But for six years running sales had been going downhill. Finally, I was called in as consultant.

At the meeting that December the sales manager was handing out the quotas amid the usual grumbling. Then one man said: "Why don't you let me work out my own sales goals? I know what I can sell in Texas and Oklahoma better than you Yankees can figure it out."

Both the sales manager and I reacted favorably, and after considerable discussion the idea took hold with everyone present. "Okay," said the manager, "you can set your own figures. You won't be working in the dark because we'll give you all the information we have available."

By the end of the month each man turned in his own sales goals. While we accepted their figures, both the sales manager and I felt they were on the high side. But the men went to work with a will—and plenty of ingenuity. For now they were dealing with their own objectives, and they had every intention of achieving them.

To begin with, each man got some of his good customers on the team by discussing with them their share of his quota. Each man furthered this team effort by doing more to help his customers move goods off their shelves. And together with the home office all worked harder to provide supplementary promotions when they were needed to go over the top.

By the end of the year each of these nine salesmen had exceeded his own bold objectives, not in every detail but in overall volume. Every December the salesmen of that firm continue to turn in their own objectives. In most cases their figures have been higher than those the home office worked out. And generally they still exceed their self-chosen goals.

Like other companies that have adopted this procedure,

the firm would not consider going back to the traditional method of assigning quotas. Nor would any of the salesmen. *Make them your own.* If your firm insists on imposing individual goals of its own choosing, you can still convert them into your own by adding goals which stamp your personal imprint on the projections. You might include such things as

Developing a plan to cultivate more prospects.
Gaining more product knowledge.
Developing more creative selling approaches.
Training the customer's sales staff to do a better job.

What corollary goals you add is for you to decide. What counts is doing it, for by personalizing management-imposed objectives you'll insure your own improved performance.

If your projections affect your earnings. Occasionally, a firm adopts the illogical practice of asking its salesmen to project their own sales objectives and then of awarding bonuses to those who achieve them. Under these conditions a salesman who makes bold projections must clearly work against his own monetary interest.

Thus he may well turn in a conservative objective. But he can still develop bold supplementary objectives strictly for personal use. By using them to guide his daily activities, he will motivate himself to higher performance levels and consequent recognition.

2 MAKE YOUR GOALS MEASURABLE

Establishing goals in terms of specific figures and dates helps you keep your work under control. You can see how much and where you must increase your efforts to realize your aims. Each new customer gained, each repeat sale,

[handwritten marginalia: "a proposition. Proven. Corollary — one already from following"]

each name added to your prospect list, is viewed as another step toward your personal target. Thus every sale stimulates additional selling efforts.

An example provides an illuminating contrast between vaguely stated goals and measurable ones. Jim Baxter, a salesman whose volume and earnings were a shade above average, had long wanted to reach the top earnings brackets. But this desire was lost in a striving for goals stated in the most general terms. Then three years ago came a dramatic change.

As he tells it: "One weekend my fishing partner could not join me. Going out alone, I began to think about my work. Although I was doing all right, I knew I had it in me to do much better. I had attended a course on management by objectives and thought I could apply it to my operation by developing definite objectives for each of my major lines and for each major account. I also developed somewhat similar figures for my target prospects and discounted the prospect totals by 66 percent, for I could not tell which ones I would or would not land.

"I considered each account objectively and evaluated its growth possibilities for my various lines. In many cases I discussed the objectives with my customers, and this served to strengthen my relationships with them.

"For some accounts I projected a probable loss in volume. But for the most part I set my sights higher: 5 percent here, 20 percent there, and 50 percent or more in other cases. But higher or lower, *I set a definite figure in each case and gave myself exactly 12 months to make good.*"

Here Jim makes a significant point: "The more specific I made each goal, the more excited I became about the potentials. It caused me to do much more constructive thinking about how these expanded goals could be reached for each customer. It all boiled down to one basic idea: How could I be more helpful to them?

"As a result, I prepared much more completely for each call. For one thing, I read technical articles more thoroughly so that I could pass along ideas which might ease a particular manufacturing problem. I took every possible opportunity to exchange ideas on machining and shaping aluminum with shop men, whether or not my products were involved. With their help I was able to spot situations where customers could use my products to advantage. On each call I had my objectives more clearly in mind.

"Using these methods, I made somewhat fewer calls. But at the end of the first year I had scored the largest increase in sales I had ever made, and by a good margin. This approach paid off even better the second year. Previously I secured a good share of my business because my prices were competitive. Now I get a much larger amount of repeat business because I paved the way with constructive approaches.

"Of course, I still go after the competitive and order-filling business. Actually, I get more of this than I did before because the more constructive approach has built up goodwill for me."

Jim draws his own moral: "I can't remember a time when I didn't want to boost my business considerably. Yet I never put concentrated push behind this vaguely stated desire. But once I had detailed figures and deadlines staring me in the face, I found myself strongly impelled to make them good. I do a better job of planning for each call; I study up on applications; I work in an extra call or two at every opportunity. Now I wouldn't dream of starting a year without first drawing up my sales objectives, complete with specific figures and deadlines."

That's the way it is. Objectives become most effective as motivators when every target is spelled out precisely. As General Electric reports: "Our records show that productivity goes up sharply when a man's efforts are directed toward specific, measurable goals." Four things in particular account for this:

> You make a deeper commitment to yourself.
> The figures and timetables give you a continuing sense of urgency.
> You get a built-in control; thus you can check your progress regularly, directing more effort when and where it is needed.
> Specific figures impel you to plan more precisely.

Put a number to it. The results of improved performance will usually show up in terms of more calls per week, more sales per call, increased volume, more sales of specific products in a line, or some other quantitative aspect. It is these expected results that make it possible to state your goals in measurable form.

Often it can be done quite simply. One wholesale lumberman set a personal objective of selling two carloads of lumber a day. This simple but highly measurable goal served to guide his every business activity. It enabled him to know just how he stood at any given moment and how much more effort he needed to go over the top. And because that specific figure kept nudging at him, he eventually made it, though he had never before come close to selling that much.

Others find it desirable to have additional breakdowns: according to each of several lines, according to units and dollars, according to customers and prospects, and so on. A building materials salesman stresses profit.

"I find it a good idea," he writes, "to establish quotas to improve my profit even more than my volume. I check my sales weekly to see where I'm tailing off. Every four months I go through each customer's invoices with an eye for items that carry larger profit. I can quickly tell what percentage of his profit business I'm getting and what I must concentrate on to increase my profit with that account. My earnings have been on an upward spiral ever since I adopted this plan."

Put a date to it, too. Don't set goals on an open-ended basis. You can rarely gain the sense of urgency needed to propel you to the finish unless you have a deadline nagging at you.

When goals require a month or more for completion, break them down into smaller, intermediate steps. A series of small successes imparts a feeling of progress and achievement, builds confidence, and expands mental horizons.

In brief, putting a number and a time to it makes your objectives more real, your plans more meaningful. You pace yourself properly; you break down your ultimate goal into easily attainable stages.

(3) AIM HIGH: PUT "STRETCH" IN YOUR GOALS

The achievement gap. That goals pave the way to success would need no further elaboration were it not for one inescapable fact. Everyone would like to make a splash in life, but few actually do.

Why this achievement gap? For one reason: we pitch too low.

We all develop habits of thought and action which reflect our self-image at any given moment. Thus our role in life is indicated by the goals we choose for ourselves.

The classic example of this phenomenon is the aptly named "underachiever," the man who falls far short of his potential. Afraid to fly high, he aspires to little more than his weekly pay check. Adjusting to the level of the limited demands he makes on himself, he stagnates in a job which no longer keeps pace with his talents.

Let him once adopt an ambitious goal, however, and he begins to act in a new manner. After lifelong study of famous men Arnold Toynbee, the noted historian, drew this conclusion: "History shows that failure can only be overcome by two things. First, a goal which takes the imagination by storm, and second, a definite and intelligible plan for carrying that goal into action."

a fixed routine, procedure etc.

Rut — way of acting ***It's all in the head***

Consider the saga of Frank Hollis, "a good man in a rut," as banker Roger Elwood phrases it.

Hollis, mortgage officer in a suburban bank where Elwood was then manager, was content with the business which found its way to his desk in the normal run of things. He did little to promote the development of new business.

"Perhaps he'd still be in that rut if two things hadn't occurred," Elwood says. "First, a savings and loan association opened an office nearby and began making heavy inroads in our mortgage business. Second, I read a management book on selling which put heavy stress on developing objectives. So I called Frank in and told him we had to do something about the S&L competition.

" 'What do you have in mind?' he asked.

"I asked him first to read the sales book. When he had finished it, I said: 'You're our mortgage expert. Could you check over our records and those of our competitors and then project a healthy increase that you might be able to swing for next year?'

Sagas — a medieval Scandinavian story telling of battles legends etc.

"It worked like a shot of adrenalin. Three weeks later he was in my office with his figures: a projected increase of 20 percent in new mortgages. What's more, he put on my desk a plan designed to gain the interest of others in our community who could be helpful. We adopted it in toto."

To begin with, Hollis initiated a monthly mailing program to builders, realtors, and contractors. Each mailing included some useful information, such as an analysis of FHA policy. To back up these mailings, he worked out a revolving schedule for another officer and himself to cultivate members of the local home builders association.

Nor was the retail side neglected. Seasonal mailings went out to all mortgage customers advising them of the possibility of refinancing their present mortgage to provide funds for remodeling, college tuition, or other needs. Local organizations were informed that upon one week's notice a bank officer could be available to speak at their meetings.

Finally, with the cooperation of several departments of the bank, Hollis met with tellers and others to show them how to refer potential mortgage prospects to the mortgage department and, if business resulted, to win both recognition and prizes.

At year's end an increase of 37 percent was recorded. Elwood congratulated the mortgage officer, remarking: "I guess your ambitious objectives really made you hustle."

"You can say that again," Hollis answered with a grin. "But hustle wasn't the main reason we pulled ahead." Pointing to his head, he said: "It was all up here. With that big 20 percent nudging me, I could no longer be satisfied with just a 'good enough' day. *I had to give one more hour to studying customer needs, to figuring out one new angle for each interview.*

"I'm going to start every year by putting down on paper the most ambitious goals I can set for myself."

How much "stretch"? Spurred on by a goal that "takes the imagination by storm," you become your own hardest taskmaster, as the italicized sentence indicates. Should the need for new skills or new knowledge emerge, the pull of a worthy aim provides the maximum incentive for taking up the slack.

Perhaps I should make one thing clear at this point. I do not say that any goal you draw up will automatically be achieved. I do say this: when you set an ambitious goal and buckle down to planning for it, talents of yours which now lie quiescent will awaken.

That's the practical content of the conclusions drawn by Dr. Kurt Lewin, founder of the Research Center for Group Dynamics at MIT. After years of studying the effects of personal and group objectives on individual performance, Dr. Lewin wrote: "Would you like your employees to do better this year than last? Simply ask them to meet 'impossible' goals.

"The successful individual sets his next goal well above his last achievement. In that way he steadily raises his level of performance."

Nearly everyone will agree that bold objectives are a tremendous stimulant, provided they are realistic. But how do you define "realistic" when the more you "stretch," the more you achieve?

Time and again I have seen salesmen project objectives which I thought were too high. Yet in a surprising number of cases they made them. And those additional and often substantial gains can be credited chiefly to the stretch they put in their objectives.

"But," some salesmen have asked me, "won't they be frustrated if they don't make their bold objectives?" One might think so. In actual practice, however, salesmen who put stretch in their goals do better than they otherwise would. Thus they are pleased, and so are their managers. Michelangelo demonstrated his complete understanding of this situation when he wrote: "Lord, grant that I may always desire more than I can accomplish."

(4) ADD ESSENTIAL COROLLARY OBJECTIVES

You'll improve your chances of achieving your bold primary objectives when you also adopt corollary goals *which apply specifically to you and to your territory.* These include:

> Increasing your knowledge of uses and applications.
> Learning more about customers' problems and business plans.
> Organizing better presentations—sometimes visual as well as oral.
> Selling in greater depth.
> Making the average call more productive.
> Selling the complete line to more customers.
> Selling more of the profitable items.
> Doing more prospecting for new accounts.
> Managing time more effectively.
> Relating effort more closely to sales potential.
> Using the telephone to greater advantage.
> Training distributors' salesmen to sell more of your items.
> Helping dealers pilot more goods off their shelves.
> Assisting customers in using your products to greater advantage.

Each representative's corollary objectives will be different. One salesman might need greater emphasis on prospecting; another may have more accounts than he can handle adequately. One may be selling products which normally affect a single department of an organization; another may have a line which should be sold in depth to the executives of more departments than he currently reaches effectively.

Each representative should adopt corollary objectives to meet his specific needs, and he should concentrate on only a limited number at a time so that he will be able to achieve them.

Note that these corollary objectives should also be subject to measurement, close enough to enable a well-organized salesman to know just where he stands and to focus on activities that need strengthening.

(5) SHARE YOUR OBJECTIVES

No salesman achieves his goals entirely by himself. In addition to his associates, his supervisor, and higher management, outside sources can provide assistance. Hence the importance of sharing objectives with others. Some people do not like to ask for help; but the fact that we all need it on occasion must be recognized.

Research on personal goal setting shows that there is no substitute for a definite statement, written or oral, in which the individual makes a commitment not only to himself but to those who depend upon his actions. This dual commitment triggers the fullest motivation.

For example, one cement salesman set a sales objective well beyond what any salesman in his company had ever achieved. For three straight years he came closer to it. And in the fourth year he made it.

Everybody knew about his objective: his fellow salesmen, his boss, his customers, his family, even some of his competitors. Without doubt, this was one of the chief reasons that his sales kept climbing year after year.

The salesman just couldn't let all those people down. Nor could he let himself down.

Spurred by the knowledge that others are watching your progress, you too will develop a momentum which seldom relaxes even after you go over the top. What's more, people respect a man who is aiming high, and they'll help you if they can. Management will lend a hand when possible; fellow workers will be happy to exchange constructive ideas and experiences. And your family and friends will offer welcome words of encouragement.

(6) PLAN TO ACHIEVE YOUR GOALS

Unless you establish sound plans to attain them, your goals may be no more than "such stuff as dreams are made on," as Shakespeare put it. The gap between aspirations and achievement can be as wide as the distance between daydreams and reality. Your plans will vary with your goals. But in every case they should be defined in action.

Take a simple illustration. Four years ago, as he contemplated the expenses of raising a growing family, wholesale salesman Bob Nash knew he had to boost his earnings drastically.

"For the first time," he says, "I *studied* my income figures. I found that for every $100 I sold on my daily rounds, I would earn commissions on $500 because repeat orders would be phoned in. I knew that I needed a daily sales average of $275 to meet my climbing expenses—much more than I had ever sold before. But it had to be done, so that became my objective.

"However, I had not thought in terms of an overall plan to implement that goal. So while I did increase my sales, I came nowhere near the figure I needed. Luckily, I attended the training session where you spoke of the need for planning to attain one's objectives. After some thought, I decided that my best plan was to concentrate on promotions that would help my customers sell more.

"To help small and medium-sized retailers capitalize on national and local advertising, I had each dealer organize a special activity to display tie-ins with current national advertising and, in some instances, with featured items of local chains. This required a lot of work each week to keep the dealers fully advised. But this and other promotion plans paid off to the extent of helping me overrun my daily sales average of $275 before the year was out."

And that was only the beginning. "The next year," Bob says, "I raised my goal, overran it again, then raised it still a third time. Now I'm up to $400 a day—and all because I no longer close up shop mentally when my last call is finished. Before I relax for the evening, I start thinking clearly about my plans for the next day's rounds and working out approaches I'm going to make to each of my customers and prospects.

"That's the main thing I have learned from these past four years. My objectives give me the push; my plans give me the means."

The moral is clear. While objectives do supply the motivating power, results do not flow automatically. Failure to plan ahead can stop the soundest goal dead in its tracks.

LIVE YOUR OBJECTIVES

The most skillful application of objectives will be essentially meaningless without consistent follow-through. And you will follow through to greatest effect when you *live your objectives,* when you know exactly where you are at any given moment and how far you must go to reach your goals. If you do not know how you are doing every working day on each of your major objectives, you are not truly living them and your progress loses momentum. Not that you must know where you stand down to the last dime, but certainly you should be aware of exactly where you must put your effort and emphasis.

The wholesale salesman whose objective was to take orders for $275 a day and the lumber salesman who was out to sell two carloads a day found it easy enough to know exactly where they stood. When you have many lines and many breakdowns, you need your monthly figures to control your plans and sales effort. But in almost all instances the interested salesman can keep close enough track to be on top of his job every day. Only then will he be truly living his objectives.

Of the seven steps that turn objectives into a powerful motivating force, living them is the most essential. For it establishes the follow-through which enables you to tap your inner resources continually year after year.

Review your goals in the light of changing conditions, perhaps once or twice a year, or more often. Revise them as needed; then change your plans accordingly. And no matter how extensive your revisions always keep your figures bold, specific, and measurable.

Most important, live your objectives on a daily basis.

BUILDING THE HABIT

You have considered the seven steps in the goal-setting process: you have set your own objectives; you have made each goal measurable; you have put stretch in your goals;

you have added corollary objectives; you have shared your goals; you have made your plans to achieve them; and you are living your objectives. The end result of this process is a set of specific targets stated in quantitative terms that channels your efforts into those activities that have the most meaning for you and your firm.

Now you're ready for your habit-building application.

What, if anything, will you plan to do as a result of your consideration of the first fundamental—your personal and sales objectives? The following questions may be useful:

1. Are you fully aware of management's overall objectives insofar as they may affect you? If not, how can you best gain further clarification?

2. Have you all the available data to assist you in developing your objectives? If not, how will you acquire them?

3. What are your long-range objectives? What are your primary objectives for the next 6 or 12 months?

4. What is the best way for you to break down your primary objectives? By volume? By profit? By lines? By months or weeks?

5. Will you measure each of your figure objectives by numbers? By dollars? By both? By profit?

6. Will you put the right amount of stretch in your objectives to make the best use of your ability? Will you develop a sufficiently definite timetable to measure your progress adequately, even if yours is a seasonal business?

7. What corollary objectives will be of considerable value in helping you achieve your figure objectives? How will you measure your progress on these corollary objectives?

8. What step-by-step process will you follow to put your territory on a management-by-objectives basis? What difficulties do you foresee and how will you plan to meet them?

9. With whom will you want to share your objectives? Who will be on your team to help you? Your manager? Advertising and promotion department? Engineering services? Distributors and their salesmen?

10. Will one of your objectives be to develop the habit of living your objectives *each day, each month, and each year?*

3

Objectives:
The Key to Direction

In Chapter 2 we examined the self-motivating power of bold long-range objectives. Here we shall focus on the selling power of your more immediate daily objectives: those which define exactly what you hope to accomplish when you are calling on a given customer or prospect.

You can best appreciate and harness this selling power by approaching it under two broad headings: (1) draw up specific objectives for each call, (2) make more constructive calls.

DRAW UP SPECIFIC OBJECTIVES FOR EACH CALL

"Isn't the primary aim of each call to land the order?" salesmen sometimes ask. Getting the business is, of course, 37 your ultimate aim for each *account*. But it cannot always be the specific aim of each *call*.

On one call you may be out to explore the customer's needs. On another you may want to help him develop a better inventory or suggest a promotion to bring in more traffic.

Whatever your specific objectives may be, when you walk in with a definite purpose, you are far more likely to walk out with a competitive advantage—if not with the sale.

Why? Because when you sharpen your objectives for each call and know exactly what you hope to accomplish, you focus all your thoughts and actions on achieving your goal.

The specific objective paid off

Consider the case of a bank officer who was making a second call on a prospect, one Richard Moore. The officer who previously serviced Mr. Moore and his firm had been trying for several years to get him to appoint the bank as executor of his estate. But Mr. Moore remained noncommittal.

On his first visit the new calling officer had also set out to have the bank chosen as executor. To this end, he had discussed some of the advantages in such a move, only to get the same inconclusive response.

On the second call he set himself a more limited objective. Rather than trying to get the prospect's full commitment, he now set his sights on one specific goal: to arrange a meeting between Mr. Moore and one of the bank's trust officers.

After some general talk, the banker asked: "Mr. Moore,

I wonder if you have given any thought to our last discussion?"

"Very little."

"Assuming you made the best possible arrangements for the administration of your estate to protect your family's interest," the officer continued very slowly, "would that give you greater peace of mind?"

Mr. Moore sat there for quite a time thinking, and the banker was careful not to interrupt his thoughts. Finally, Mr. Moore said softly: "It might."

"Do you think your family would feel more secure?"

Mr. Moore nodded.

"Then would it make sense to look into the means for making such an arrangement?"

"I suppose it would."

"Since you see it that way," the officer said, "I would like you to meet Mr. Grant, a senior trust officer. If you will check your appointment book, I can arrange a convenient time for you."

"I'll be in tomorrow morning at 9:30," Mr. Moore replied.

A few days later, while details were being worked out, Mr. Moore's attorney asked the officer: "How did you ever persuade Mr. Moore to take this step? I've been trying to get him to make up his mind for over two years, and I know your predecessor was working on it too."

"By approaching him with but one aim in mind," said the officer. "Many men shy away from this decision," he continued, "and sometimes until it is too late. I thought it was time to take one small step. *That was the sole objective of my visit.* Everything I said was carefully thought out to help him do just one thing—come in and talk it over.

"Of course," he told the lawyer, "your groundwork and that of my predecessor were key factors. *But having a highly specific aim laid the foundation for achieving it.* Instead of dissipating my energies by trying to get him to agree to an estate plan, I focused my attention on one thing only: selling an appointment."

What this banker accomplished could probably have been done long ago if either the attorney or the previous calling officer had sharpened his objectives and followed through effectively, as the younger officer did.

SHARPEN YOUR OBJECTIVES FOR EACH CONTACT

It is essential to sharpen your objectives for each contact. Before you make a telephone call, for example, be sure you know exactly what you want to accomplish. Maybe your primary objective is to arrange an appointment with a prospect; you have been in the prospect's office before and know that his door is open to anyone in the plant who wants to come in and ask questions. This is not the best setting for the important presentation you have in mind. So your corollary objective is to have him meet you at a place conducive to uninterrupted conversation. To achieve your corollary objective you select, if at all possible, a spot for lunch which is interesting enough to have extra pulling power.

SELLING IN DEPTH

Often a sale rests upon a series of buying decisions from several departments and levels of command. When negotiating such a sale, a salesman must work out different objectives for each man he sees.

Take John Hunter, who was calling on a manufacturer

of equipment for the crude oil industry that used the kind of welding electrodes his firm produced.

Knowing that the company was well satisfied with its present sources, John had a limited goal when he first called upon the purchasing department: to sell the desirability of having another thoroughly reliable source on tap as an emergency measure.

With the engineering department, John took an entirely different tack. There he set out to prove that his firm could design electrodes to the prospect's exacting specifications and maintain accurate quality control in every manufacturing stage.

With top management, his aim shifted once more. At that level he had to demonstrate that his products and services could cut costs and have a favorable effect on profits.

"I would get nowhere fast," said John, "if I didn't carefully shape my sales talk to the man or men I am going to see. By working out a different objective for each department, I can slant my presentation accordingly."

MAKE MORE CONSTRUCTIVE CALLS

Every survey on the subject—and many have been made —indicates that businessmen often resent calls which have no other purpose than to maintain contact or press for another order. The customer or prospect may not express his annoyance directly; unfortunately, it may be reflected in his turning down a bid for business.

This one-sided approach can all too easily deteriorate into just another "here I am again" call (to use Professor Dick Borden's wonderfully expressive phrase). Such calls have little impact because, as one Million Dollar Club salesman shrewdly remarked, "The prospect is far more interested in his needs than in our sales pitches. As for myself, I never walk in on a prospect without some useful idea that I feel will be of service to the fellow I'm calling on."

The aim's the thing

Once they put their minds to it, most salesmen can find some valuable idea for almost every prospect or customer. One representative had a customer who used a considerable amount of hardwood flooring for commercial and institutional buildings. However, because the firm's credit line was limited, it could not make the most of its opportunities in that field.

The salesman had always figured it wasn't his headache. But on the heels of an O PIB'ROC training session he adopted the objective of making every call a constructive one. Reviewing the situation, he made it his business to find out more about the dealer's needs than he had known before.

"With this new information under my belt," the salesman says, "I helped develop a shipping schedule so that the material would arrive within a few days of the requirements of the job. The customer no longer had to tie up his operating capital with a large inventory, and he was able to discount our bills."

Up to this time the flooring had been a highly competitive item. But the salesman's constructive approach froze out the competition, and the business has continued to be highly profitable both for the salesman and for his customer.

When you do something extra for your prospect or customer—when you help him merchandise your goods better, give him helpful tie-in suggestions, give him useful applications information, help him increase store traffic, or help him make an unusual saving or record an extra gain—then you have made a constructive call.

And as you step up your percentage of such calls, doors will open more readily for you—especially on repeat sales. Calling with some constructive purpose in mind lays the foundation for building a favored position.

SERVICING AND CONTACT CALLS

Sometimes you must call to service an account or to protect it by maintaining contact. But why not make such calls do double duty by adding some constructive intent?

J. Sydney Johnson, former merchandising manager of the National Biscuit Company, underscores this point. One of the company's salesmen showed a customer how he could move biscuits and other food items faster by displaying the biscuits with related foods. The pleased customer thereupon sat down and wrote National Biscuit as follows:

"This morning 15 salesmen called on me before your man dropped in. Not one of the first 15 gave me a merchandising idea. They talked advertising, quoted prices, and showed their product, but they didn't give me a single selling idea I could use in my business. When your man showed me how I could display some of your biscuits with related foods, it was like a breath of fresh air."

No doubt about it—that salesman made a regular customer.

Two cautions. Constructive calls, as we have seen, have a powerful impact. But be sure to offer all your suggestions thoughtfully and tactfully. A prospect may be offended by "someone who thinks he knows more about my business than I do," as one dealer put it.

In addition, recognize that your objective and his interests must be closely related. If your objective is to demonstrate means of cutting his labor costs, you are both on the same wavelength. The same is true if your call has been planned to improve turnover on a specific item or line. But if your objective is to put on a promotion which will stimulate more store traffic when your customer hasn't the personnel to handle the extra flow, then you're at cross-purposes with him, which means you had best alter your objective or establish a corollary one. This could be to help him find the right personnel or to help him train present employees so that they can sell more effectively.

DEVELOPING CONSTRUCTIVE IDEAS

I have had the opportunity to work with scores of sales groups. Despite some skepticism at the start, they have all agreed after thoughtful discussion that by working out a constructive goal in advance they can call on practically every customer or prospect with the conviction that they can be of help to him.

Now where can you dig up constructive ideas? Your company can undoubtedly give you a number of them; fellow salesmen can suggest others. You can dig out many suggestions from old customers; you can get ideas from trade papers; you can ask questions of people you meet; you can watch the ads for promotional ideas.

A few examples will demonstrate the point in action and may stimulate your own thinking along these lines.

Provide tie-in suggestions to build related-item sales. One salesman suggested that a supermarket place a shelf display of salad dressing at the back of a produce case.

Though offered as a temporary promotion, the display has become a permanent fixture, since it sells 20 cases a week.

Give your customer detailed ideas on how your products can be used to best advantage. A representative of a manufacturer of molded rubber and plastic products uses a Polaroid camera to photograph finished parts and parts in process. Each photo shows a unique feature which will be of interest to specific prospects.

Show a dealer how he can increase his store traffic. In Texas, where there are a number of exclusive toy stores, one representative sold his customer on the pulling power of candy. Those stores which put in a line of candy found that it brought in youngsters and their parents. The increased traffic boosted their toy sales.

Demonstrate how your customer can make better use of goods or services, either yours or others. A salesman for a company which produces and packages bottled gas showed his distributors how they and their customers in turn could improve their efficiency by operating with a series of pre-planned purchases. This reduced the inventory of both distributors and dealers and also cut down on his own company's capital investment in pressure tanks.

Show a dealer how he can significantly increase his sales of a specific line. The representative of an ice cream manufacturer found that some supermarkets with good ice cream programs sold 2 percent and sometimes as high as 3 percent of their total volume in ice cream.

Yet other stores that had no such program but that were in a position to do as well took in as little as .5 percent of their total volume in ice cream. These important facts opened the door for him to present a total ice cream program designed to step up both volume and profit margins—all resulting in substantial added business.

"A helping frame of mind"

Usually you will plan your constructive approach in advance. But when you aim for it consciously, you will often find yourself responding more surely when fortune opens a door. Harold Lamont, a manufacturer's representative, is completely sold on the idea of constructive objectives for each call. He tells an instructive story in this regard.

"I arranged an appointment with an engineer who told me he was planning to organize a company for the manufacture and installation of water purification equipment. To open the door to this account, I determined to find some way of being constructive.

"While waiting in the office of another customer, I spotted an engineering magazine devoted to municipal water supply. Thumbing through the publication, I found an article describing a new economical process for spreading a protective film over reservoir water.

"I had that article Xeroxed. When I called on my engineer prospect and presented the copy to him, he was delighted. And the sale practically closed itself."

Salesman Lamont then underlines the moral. "Of course," he says, "I didn't plan this approach; spotting the magazine was sheer luck. But what I did about it was not chance. *For I would never have picked up that magazine had I not been alerted to every constructive possibility by my calling objective.* If it hadn't been that article," he concludes, "I'm sure I would have found something else. Aiming to make each call constructive keeps me on my toes and *puts me in a helping frame of mind.*"

BUILDING THE HABIT

As a salesman, you can increase your volume and earnings by making your objectives for each call both highly specific and constructive. To be sure, your goals may change as your prospect reacts to your presentation. But they will still raise your ratio of sales to calls by putting you in a helping frame of mind.

For each major account and prospect consider everything you hope to accomplish in the next year or in the next few months. You may find it helpful to put your account objectives in writing.

Sometime before each call determine your objectives. Endeavor to lift your sights—to plan to accomplish more than what first came to mind.

Before picking up the phone, pause long enough to be sure you have in mind all you wish to accomplish.

Building the objectives habit requires no new practice. However, by keeping it in mind you do it more consistently, more intensively, and more effectively. And you do it consciously.

Do this for a month and you will recognize that you are getting tangible gains. You will be accomplishing more than you expected to. You will appreciate that you are building an unusually valuable habit.

4

Preparation:

The Key to More Productive Presentations

Why does one man make a sale and another fail?

Let a buyer answer that one. Responding to a survey in *Purchasing* magazine, the director of purchasing for U.S. Steel put it this way: "One word is the key to why one man makes the sale when the other man doesn't: 'preparation.'" The salesman who makes the sale is the one who is prepared to give the buyer all the information he needs to buy intelligently.

THE EXTRA STEP

Every salesman prepares to some extent. But the whole point of the principle of preparation is to be so conscious of it, to apply it so thoroughly and consistently, that you go one step further than you otherwise would—the step that gives you a *competitive edge.*

That's exactly how business equipment and systems salesman George Canfield stays ahead of the flock. In this extremely competitive field large sales ride on every interview. The man who does the best job of preparing himself for the initial call has the best chance to get the order.

"You can't get anywhere in this field," says Canfield, "unless you pick up a load of background facts before you call. Many of us entertain executives from the prospect's firm as part of our fact-finding ritual. But I find that I can often come up with useful information by going beyond the usual sources and taking a lower-level employee to lunch."

Once, for example, he scouted an important prospect for a week before he made his initial call. By chatting with one of the bookkeepers at lunch, he discovered that the accounting department was working overtime all that week. Digging deeper, he found that this happened almost every month because of the type of calculating machines used. "That was all the clue I needed to prepare my approach," Canfield remarks.

"When I finally called on my prospect, I had a plan based on his problem and backed by actual figures. The plan had saved six firms in his industry up to $300 a month in labor costs alone by drastically reducing the amount of overtime needed."

Sure enough, that extra bit of preparation tipped the balance in his favor. With one more call, after getting some additional information the prospect wanted, Canfield started a new account.

How the habit of preparation can increase your sales volume will become clear as we analyze two general areas of application: (1) preparing for competition, and (2) taking the time to prepare.

PREPARING FOR COMPETITION

Most salesmen are well briefed on the need to know their competition and on strategies to meet price competition and the like. But the most neglected area—and thus the most fruitful one for the salesman who focuses on it—is the trick of gaining a competitive advantage via an extra preparatory step. This extra step of preparation can take many forms, three of which have proved especially productive:

Preparing constructive contacts.
Preparing your presentation strategy.
Acquiring more practical knowledge.

PREPARING CONSTRUCTIVE CONTACTS

In the chapter on objectives we considered the sales-building power of aiming for more constructive calls. Here we shall center on the equally important step of preparing such calls. The groundwork for most constructive contacts can be laid before you walk in the door. And the more information you gather beforehand, the better your chances of making a telling—and selling—presentation.

This is not merely a matter of theory. In response to one business publication survey, the purchasing agent of a leading paint manufacturer wrote: "I am constantly amazed that so many salesmen who call on me know so little about my firm. They want me to buy, but they don't even take the trouble to find out how their products might be of service to us. They seldom get an order."

Note the phrase "they don't even take the trouble." It cropped up again and again in this study, revealing a deepseated resentment of salesmen who don't consider the customer's needs important enough to study beforehand. Preparing a constructive contact helps you focus the interview on issues of immediate interest to your prospect.

Simply does it

Fortunately, gaining a competitive edge by preparing a constructive contact doesn't necessarily require an expensive "extra." Sometimes it means no more than taking the obvious step that your competitors may ignore precisely because it is so obvious.

For example, a new business moving into a community often touches off competition for the account among local banks. And at times, as one officer discovered, the only extra preparation needed to come out ahead is the simple yet too often overlooked step of obtaining a Dun & Bradstreet report.

"A specialty store chain, headquartered in New York, was establishing a branch at the new Fairfield Mall in our city," this banker reports. "Before making my initial contact, I ordered a D&B report and observed a cash position of $170,000, a better than two-to-one current ratio, and over $260,000 in net worth.

"I telephoned the president and outlined the many services we could offer a business of his type. When he stated that he might be in the market for some bank financing, I remarked that the firm was in good condition for it financially.

" 'How do you know so much about my business?' he wanted to know.

" 'We always research our prospects so that we can analyze their needs,' I told him.

" 'That's what I like,' he replied, 'a progressive banker who takes the trouble to research his clients.' Without further ado he told me we could count on being the bank of deposit for his new store. And he made an appointment to see me the following week to talk over the company's financing plans."

The interesting thing in this case was that the prospect was sold merely by the promise of constructive contacts by a banker "who takes the trouble" to study his clients' needs.

Even when your products or services have no direct bearing on the situation, a constructive approach can be of help to your prospect or customer and can create a climate conducive to landing an order or increasing your volume. And often enough you need only employ the habit of keeping your eyes and ears open, as the next two cases indicate.

He takes the time to read

Bernard Adamson, who sells accounting services, keeps a step ahead of his competitors by scanning newspapers and professional literature for information and ideas that might be useful to his prospects. Because of this preparation, he can often engage a prospect's interest immediately by dropping a constructive bit of news into a brief introductory remark—as he did on a recent call to an insurance broker.

"Mr. Nash, I dropped by today to tell you about a state law which was passed yesterday. Wherever you do your banking, you should open a separate insurance premium checking account."

At this, the broker perked up his ears. "What's it all about? I haven't had time to read the papers today."

"I know how it is," Adamson said sympathetically. "But keeping up with such things is part of my business." He went on to explain the law more thoroughly and how an insurance premium account would protect the broker's interests. And he walked out with an appointment to discuss his own services in two days' time. Once again, a constructive contact paved the way to a sale.

He queries other customers

Ralph Hodges, who sells a line of precision tools, had one customer, the plant manager of a hardware manufacturer, who bought from him sporadically. For a long time the manager had been disturbed over his growing costs, which stemmed in large measure from one fact: the firm bought and stored a large variety of special materials differing only in slight particulars. Hodges had been vaguely aware of this; but since the problem had no direct tie-in to his own line, he had never concerned himself with it.

Considering the situation more seriously now, Hodges decided to query other customers who were not in competition with this one. When he picked up what he felt was a sound idea, he arranged to discuss the matter with the plant manager. Following through, the manager reduced his inventory from 360 to 254 items. This move enabled him to buy in larger quantities at better prices. In addition, it increased the turnover and reduced the clerical work for buying, recording, and inventorying.

Hodges, who subsequently became the prime supplier for his grateful customer, underlines the point himself. "Formerly I merely took an active interest in those problems directly tied to my products. Now I look around for ways to help my prospect even when there are no such ties. In several cases this constructive preparation has practically ruled out competitive bids."

PREPARING YOUR PRESENTATION STRATEGY

The most productive presentations rarely if ever rest on sudden inspiration. Mostly they're planned in advance. As the famed British statesman David Lloyd George once wrote: "The surest road to inspiration is preparation."

Preparing your strategy before seeing a given contact makes a lot of sense. Indeed, it can often be the deciding factor in winning or maintaining an account.

At a meeting with his sales staff one top sales manager put it this way: "We must assume that our most worthwhile prospects and customers are being solicited by our competition. They have heard all the standard sales arguments; so if we merely duplicate the strategy our competitors use, our lack of imagination will have a negative effect."

Strategy opens the door

Hal Farmer was out to sell a line of valves to a candy manufacturer that had used another brand for years. As his first step in breaking through those long-closed doors, Hal set himself the goal of obtaining a trial order. Although his prospect was satisfied with the competing line, Hal knew from his visits to other customers that leaky valves were apt to be a problem. Accordingly, he centered his presentation strategy around a dramatic, well-prepared demonstration of the rugged strength of his own product.

When he was ready, he arranged to see the master mechanic at the main plant. After some casual chatting, he asked the man forthrightly: "Are you ever bothered by leaky valves in your operation?"

"Yes," the mechanic said. "But the chief engineer does the buying; talk to him."

Ignoring this, Hal went on. "But where do leaky valves give you the most trouble?"

"On our caramel steam kettles," the mechanic said. "But I don't do the buying," he repeated.

Hal took out one of his valves and smashed a paper clip between the seat and the disc. "Did you ever see a valve take such punishment without showing it?"

"Well, no." For the first time the prospect said nothing about not being the buyer.

"What size valves do you use on these kettles?"

"Three-quarter-inch."

"Would the ¾-inch hard-hearted valves I just demonstrated take any more punishment from your kettle than it took in smashing that clip?"

"I doubt it."

"Would it make sense to put in a requisition for some trial valves to see if they work as well as this one did?"

"I guess it would."

"If you write out a requisition for a couple of ¾-inch hard-hearted valves, can you get an order from your purchasing agent?"

The master mechanic nodded. More to the point, he went to the purchasing agent's office then and there and got the order for the trial.

By preparing an imaginative presentation strategy and following through with a fine job of selling, Hal did in a few minutes what his predecessor hadn't been able to accomplish in several years.

Winning a three-way competition

One example illustrating the power of preplanned presentation strategy occurred when I was the prospect. I asked three printers to give me quotes on a complex printing job involving a set of insurance booklets. Varying quantities were to be shipped to several thousand insurance agents throughout the country. Each order required a different imprint, and the orders and reorders would be coming in for some time.

The three shops did equally fine work, and the bids they offered were almost identical. But one printer went to the trouble of checking on exactly how the booklets were to be used.

With this information in hand, that printer made it easy for me to grasp his quotations. He organized his presentation in such a manner that I could take in almost at a glance the breakdowns required for my office to figure and quote its resale prices.

A small difference? Yes. But that extra bit of preparation landed the order. And because that start sold me on him, I have given that printer many thousands of dollars' worth of business since then.

ACQUIRING MORE PRACTICAL KNOWLEDGE

Most salesmen are well prepared as far as product knowledge goes. But unfortunately knowing your products or services doesn't go far enough. The salesman who wants to boost his sales and earnings must also know the special circumstances of each customer. For no two are alike.

In short, when you look at the subject from the buyer's

point of view—which is the view that overlooks the dotted line—it is *practical knowledge* that counts. The salesman who knows his products and can apply that knowledge to suit each customer is far ahead of the game.

He did his homework

Once you start thinking in terms of applications, product knowledge transforms itself into something much broader—and infinitely more exciting. Anthony Belli, the purchasing agent of a food processing firm, tells an instructive story in this regard.

"I give a large volume of business to one lumber salesman in particular. Why? Because he prepares his offerings in terms of our requirements.

"I remember the first time he called on me to suggest dry spruce for crating. Right off the reel he told me that spruce is especially well suited for food containers because it is tasteless and odorless. In addition, it is white and clean with little tendency to stain, thus giving an excellent quality appearance.

"He then pointed out that spruce is strong enough to handle all our packing needs, yet it is 12 to 30 percent lighter than other commonly used crating lumber. When I spoke of the size of our crates, he worked it out for me right on the spot in terms of cost and wastage.

"Now there's a man who's done his homework, I thought. If he's gone to the trouble of finding out what's best for this end use, he'll probably be equally helpful on all our lumber needs. So I gave him my first order. Later, when I found that his figures were on the conservative side, I decided to do business with him regularly."

In short, when a salesman deepens his practical knowledge and studies the ground, he sells as the customer wants to be sold.

One preparation—50 installations

How much time you put into preparing broader applications knowledge is a matter of individual judgment. Not only the present order but the future potential must be weighed.

Only you can decide. But remember: the extra step that goes into such preparation can spell the difference between moving up into the higher brackets and staying down with the crowd. This is especially true when you consider that the time you put into one preparation often pays off in multiple sales, for many situations can be applied or adapted to the needs of other prospects.

"I have made a survey of water rates in my territory," writes Manny Gordon, who sells air-conditioning systems, "and I can cite operating costs on all water-cooled equipment. I have also trained myself to become expert in the selection, piping, and control of multicircuited condensers.

"All this extra work began as part of my preparation for landing one of my biggest contracts in the face of strong competition. Because of this background knowledge, I have since sold over 50 similar installations with little or no additional effort."

Every salesman has numerous sources: his sales manager, his fellow salesmen, his training director, catalogs, sales manuals, company literature, home office personnel, servicemen, engineers, trade literature, courses, books. But not all salesmen make the most of those sources.

Two things are needed for this: a strong desire to improve your practical knowledge and a definite plan. You can broaden your information backlog for preparing constructive contacts and improving strategy in these three ways:

Building the inquiring-eye habit.
Reading, studying, and attending meetings.
Organizing your reference material.

BUILDING THE INQUIRING-EYE HABIT

One forward-thinking young man in the highly competitive field of lubricating oils has decided views on how to keep a big jump ahead of his competitors. "As I see it," he says, "there is only one way you can sell more than the next man: you have to find more and better ways to use your products profitably."

He never lets a day go by without picking up some practical information. Whenever he visits a plant, he keeps a careful eye out for new uses of different lubricants. Almost always he sees something worth inquiring about.

Sometimes he may not get an immediate answer to his questions. In that case he jots them down in a pocket notebook he carries around for that purpose. Then, when the chance presents itself, he ferrets out the information from various sources. In this way he has gradually become a walking encyclopedia of useful knowledge.

"I ask questions of maintenance men, shop men, and engineers. If an idea sounds promising, I put it into my notebook. Most of what I pick up in this way comes in handy.

"For example, when I made my first call on a builder

of diesel engines, I brought along a detailed chart showing how lubricants could be specified for each type of engine the builder manufactured. My prospect had in mind only a small order when I called; but my chart gave him the idea of printing the information for his complete line in the booklet he now gives to his customers. As a result, we now supply nearly all his lubricating needs.

"The point is simple. Without my questions, no notes. Without my notes, no chart. And without my chart, no big sale.

"I now have several dozen of these notebooks. I review one or two every week to keep this valuable data in mind so that I can make good use of it practically every day I am calling on customers or prospects.

"It's the most profitable thing I've ever done. Many times these information books have helped me win against the toughest competition."

READING, STUDYING, AND ATTENDING MEETINGS

Every industry piles up its quota of literature. But this reservoir of knowledge is useful to the individual salesman only to the extent that he dips into and uses it.

The problem is how to read it all.

The answer is: you can't. No matter how much time you have squeezed out for it, there is usually far more to read than you can thoughtfully review.

But consider. Most of us have the same problem with prospects. We have far more than we can possibly reach effectively.

What do we do in that case?

We use some sort of cream-separating device. Then we concentrate on the best.

You can plan your reading, studying, and going to meetings on an equally selective basis.

How one man does it

One successful manufacturer's agent who must keep up with a number of different technical lines does just that. First he divides his reading material into three piles: "must read," "read if possible," and "throw out."

Then he stacks the "must read" and "read if possible" items into first-things-first sequence, taking each in turn and reading it slowly or skimming it rapidly according to its importance.

For example, assuming he has placed a dozen bulletins and two books on his "must read" pile, he takes just one bulletin and reads it, or part of it, thoughtfully. Then he considers where and how he can use the data. If he knows someone who is quite familiar with the subject, he plans to discuss it with him further. When he is sure he has these major points pat, then—and only then—does he take on the next bulletin.

Some items he clips, some he makes notes on; then he files them in well-indexed folders. And he follows the same method to absorb technical or applications knowledge more easily and thoroughly. In this manner he finds that he can actually absorb considerably more practical knowledge than ever before and in much less time.

Speed reading. Numerous tests indicate that the average American reads between 225 and 275 words a minute. In grade school most of us learned to read one word at a time, and that is what we have done ever since.

President Kennedy found himself in that situation. So he attended a few speed-reading classes and then continued to practice on his own. At the time he started he read about 250 words a minute. With practice he increased his speed to 1,200 words a minute with proportionate increases in absorption and retention.

In meetings with forward-looking groups of sales managers, I have often asked how many have studied speed reading. About one in five has been the response. Of these, 80 to 90 percent say that it has been very helpful to them.

By enrolling in speed-reading courses or by practicing on your own with the help of a good text, you can expect to at least *double* your reading speed. And remember: as so many salesmen have demonstrated, the more information you pick up by reading or study, the more sales you will record.

Think "applications"

How much you read is not the point. What counts most is applying what you have learned. You can start this even during the reading session. Read a bit. Then pause and think about where and how you can apply this knowledge.

If you want to apply your goods and services to the needs of your customers and prospects, watch their operations. How do they go about moving your goods off their shelves? Just how do they use your products in their manufacturing operations? With such knowledge in hand, you will be in a much better position to help them and others see the advantages of your products and services.

ORGANIZING YOUR REFERENCE MATERIAL

It is one thing to be exposed to useful knowledge. It is still another to have that knowledge on tap when and where you need it.

Some facts you can keep in your head. In many instances, however, you are exposed to much more useful knowledge than you can possibly keep in mind.

How one man solved this problem

Organizing such data in a form that you can use promptly and effectively requires real thought and ingenuity. Over a period of time one man accumulated several thousand clippings, bulletins, technical papers, references to specific passages, and books. Much of this literature touched upon several subjects.

After considerable thought, he listed 28 broad topics which became the main divisions of his subject filing. Each of these topics in turn had subdivisions.

As he reads a bulletin, he uses distinctive underlining to identify subtopics, and if necessary he notes the pertinent major heading. Then he makes several copies of the bulletin, filing one under each subtopic.

"Has it been worth the effort?" I asked this man.

He replied: "This file time and again has enabled me to speak authoritatively upon scores of process engineering problems. It has been a significant factor in helping me to sell a number of substantial contracts for my firm.

"It does take time and effort, but in the long run it probably saves at least as much time and effort. And even if it took five times longer than it does, it would still pay off manyfold."

Few representatives have need for such a wide range of reference information. But many a sale will be saved if you organize your reference material in as effective a manner, so you can put your finger on the required knowledge when you need it.

Make constructive use of your knowledge

When you know your customers' problems and apply your knowledge to help solve those problems, you are using your knowledge most constructively. More to the point, the practical application of product and customer knowledge will be clearly reflected in your sales and earnings.

Taking the Time to Prepare

"The hardest thing about preparation," writes one salesman, "is finding the time for it. However, if you don't take the time beforehand, *you waste it when making the call.*"

Another man lays the problem right on the line: "A seven-hour day spent calling on clients should be preceded by a couple of hours of preparation the night before. Like most salesmen, I often find this impossible to do. But I can say without question that my most profitable days on the road always come when I manage to spend some time on preparation the night before."

He takes a mental trip

"My personal approach to preparation," an industrial salesman writes, "is to devote some free moments of a Sunday afternoon or evening to random thoughts of the week's coming trip. I take a mental trip through my territory, thinking of each buyer in the order in which I'll probably see him and reviewing, with the aid of a notebook designed for this purpose, our last conversation. With each one I make two specific checks:

"Checkpoint 1: 'Did I promise in our last session any quotation, information, or servicing that I have not yet provided?' If so, I make sure I have the material or information on hand for the coming trip.

"Checkpoint 2: 'What basic new points of information have I picked up in the past two or three weeks that will be of interest to my customer—points I should stress on my call this week? What should I try to sell this week—or should I just plant the seed for a future sale?' My answers all go down in my notebook under that buyer's name. Even in a slow time of the year, when the chances for sales are slim, I try to show some ideas that will impress the customer with my desire to be a service-minded salesman instead of just another order taker."

While this salesman prepares for his week's calls on Sunday, others prefer to prepare for each day's calls the night before. However and whenever he does it, one thing is certain: the salesman who goes to bed knowing on whom he plans to call and what he plans to cover with each contact the next day will make more effective presentations and write more orders than the salesman who has not done such preplanning.

What time you choose doesn't matter. What counts is developing the habit of setting aside some regular time for preparation. It is a habit that pays handsome dividends.

BUILDING THE HABIT

As with objectives, building the preparation habit involves no break with old practices. Rather, it means giving conscious attention to consistent application during the habit-forming month. To this end, you can follow a rough-and-ready guide. Before you walk in on a customer or prospect, consider the following points:

1. Are you prepared to make a constructive contact? Do you know the specific needs of the prospect or customer you will see? Can you give him a clear picture of how you can serve his needs?
2. Have you worked out an overall presentation strategy? Do you know how your prospect plans to use your product or service? Can you show him how he can best adapt your product to his uses? Have you prepared a specific offering geared to his needs?
3. If there's competition in the picture, can you point to something that gives you a competitive edge? Can you demonstrate the superiority of your product in a way that will let it speak for itself?
4. Have you rehearsed your demonstrations so that you can give them without fumbling?

When your answers to such questions come up no, take the extra steps required to transform them to yes. That's how you build the habit of preparation—the key to more productive presentations.

5

Inquiry:
The Key to Your Prospect's Interest

No matter how well you prepare, there are bound to be blind spots in your knowledge of a given prospect's needs. The best way to remove them is to inquire, to ask questions designed to arouse interest and to uncover those selling points that the prospect finds most attractive. And the more pains you take with queries that are obviously meant for the prospect's benefit, *the more he will tend to sell himself on the desirability of dealing with you.*

Every salesman inquires to some extent; he wouldn't do much business otherwise. But when a salesman concentrates on the principle of inquiry, he asks more questions—and more penetrating ones. It is this extra concentration which leads to extra sales.

A SOFT-SELL PATTERN

Analyze any example of thoughtful inquiry and a distinctive soft-sell pattern emerges. One question shows an interest in the prospect; another draws out a key fact about his needs; a third underscores a major benefit; a fourth suggests specific competitive advantages for the job at hand; a fifth leads the prospect gently to the dotted line.

The distinct advantages of the soft-sell, preplanned line of inquiry will be demonstrated quite clearly as we consider the five broad, somewhat overlapping applications of this principle:

> Use "door openers": inquiry as attention getter.
> Dig out the key selling points.
> Plant the seed of desire.
> Tackle the competition diplomatically.
> Help the prospect sell himself.

These techniques require a certain amount of finesse. The best way to acquire them is to analyze the good and not so good examples of inquiry given below.

USE "DOOR OPENERS": INQUIRY AS ATTENTION GETTER

Many prospects automatically put up their guard when a salesman appears on the scene. Sure, they'll listen—with one ear, and one eye on the clock.

You can improve your chances of a sale if you can win the prospect's undivided attention with a "door opener," an opening shot which arouses interest and gets you heard. Not that you need to set off a string of firecrackers to announce your presence. *Just address a query directly to the prospect's needs, desires, or general business interests.* It's truly as simple as that.

Indeed, the biggest mistake in selling is to look at your story from your point of view. At the point of sale the prospect's perspective takes precedence.

Before and after: a matter of perspective

When calling on an agent, insurance adjuster George Manning opened fire like this: "Mr. Blake, our records show that we've been getting a good share of your assignments, but practically all of it has been on casualty and auto claims. Of course, we appreciate the business, *but we want to develop more growth in fire and allied lines.* I'd like to go into that with you today."

"Make it some other time, will you? I'm too busy now."

The italicized phrase is a good—or rather, a horrible—example of the self-centered approach a salesman may slip into unawares. Why should a prospect jump for joy because you "want to develop . . ."?

See what happened, instead, when a salesman tackled the same issue in query form, avoiding the self-centered tone by asking a you-minded question. "Mr. Blake, while I was waiting in your office I picked up one of your advertising folders. I take it that fast and efficient loss service is the heart of your business."

"Are you kidding? I couldn't stay ahead of the game without it."

"Then let me ask you this: Did you ever stop to think that with our countrywide organization we can do a better job for your insureds, boost your reputation, and give you the same competitive edge on fire and allied claims that we now give you on casualty and auto losses?"

"How can you boost my reputation?"

This question demonstrates that the salesman's door-opening query achieved its goal. For now the agent was *listening*. And the more a prospect listens, the more he'll buy.

Note how the salesman zeroed in on the agent's main interests with the statement "I take it that . . . ," which is in itself an implied question. Then he underlined his you-minded approach by casting a promise of gain in query form. This had the added virtue of softening what might otherwise seem to be somewhat brash claims.

Nor was all this accidental. For the same salesman was involved in both cases. After analyzing the rebuff to his original presentation, George Manning was well motivated to sit down and prepare this far more effective door opener.

PREPARE YOUR OWN QUESTIONS

One salesman, for example, initiates a sale by asking directly: "Do you know that these wrapping machines will give you at least 10 percent more output than you are now getting—and with much less maintenance cost?"

In this manner he arouses the prospect's interest. And the prospect is almost bound to say yes when the salesman then asks: "Would you like me to show you some comparative figures?"

The salesman reports that his batting average has improved since he changed from the flat statement "These wrapping machines will give you . . ." to a soft-sell inquiry.

But *don't* trust to on-the-spot inspiration. *Do* prepare some of your questions beforehand.

The most effective door openers are those slanted specifically at a given prospect. With sufficient thought, any salesman can prepare himself with a good stock of queries suited to varying circumstances. For example: "Would you be interested in an idea that can save storage space?" "Are you concerned with increasing store traffic?"

You don't have to search for clever questions. Just prepare them in advance, keep them you-minded, and preface each query with a remark that shows the probe is in the prospect's interest, not yours.

Dig Out the Key Selling Points

If you're starting cold or with only a partial clue to your prospect's needs, you can dig out the rest during your interview—if you've prepared a sufficient stock of questions beforehand. And as one experienced salesman notes: "Inquiry is the perfect soft-sell way of pinpointing the main selling points." Consider the following case.

"How many cans do you sell?"

George Lister, a wonderfully good candy salesman, had a dollar seller which turned over rapidly when a retailer put it on the counter in the cardboard display which was supplied with each order for three dozen boxes or more.

Hearing his story, a prospect would often say: "It sounds fine. But as you can see, I have no space to display another item."

After encountering this situation a number of times, George prepared an information-probing line of inquiry. On almost every call he had spotted a couple of displays which he thought might be replaced with his. To lead to that point, he prepared a question aimed directly at the prospect's business interests. Here's how it worked in a typical case.

"How many cans of lighter fluid do you sell from that display?" he asked a druggist.

"Maybe three or four a day," replied the proprietor.

"How much profit do you make?"

"About 40 cents."

"Would you sell some if you didn't have them on the counter?"

"Maybe half."

"Then that display space now yields about 20 cents a day. Is that right?"

"I guess so."

"Would you like to increase the yield from that same space to over a dollar?" asked George.

"I sure would."

After citing a couple of stores which had used his display for some time, George asked: "Do you think you have as much traffic as either of those stores?"

"Probably more," said the proprietor.

"Well, the first store I mentioned is averaging a little better than two boxes a day. And the second store is doing almost three. So would it seem fair to say that you would probably average two and a half?"

"That seems reasonable."

"The profit per box is 40 cents. Two and a half boxes a day would yield a profit of a dollar. That is approximately five times what you are now making from that space. Instead of realizing $73 in profit per year, you would make $365. Would you like to take in almost $300 more a year just by changing displays?"

Of course, George made that sale. And he makes

enough others with his door-opening queries to keep him in a high-income bracket. Commenting on this experience, George remarked: "Before I fully absorbed the principle of inquiry, I limited myself to a few leading questions. All too often I failed to get to the heart of the prospect's problems. Nor could I guide his thinking along lines which could benefit him and my company.

"Now I sometimes work out as many as 12 or 15 questions when preparing for a call. I may not use them all. I may even change the 'script' entirely if something new comes up. But however the interview goes, inquiry helps me keep on top of the situation."

A WORD ABOUT TACT

Every salesman must, of course, exercise tact at all times, especially when probing deeply. Given common sense and a friendly tone, however, inquiry will rarely if ever cause resentment. On the contrary, when you set out to be helpful, that desire will shine through.

One salesman puts the point well: "I am fully convinced that if you will take the trouble to prepare questions pertaining to a prospect's needs, you can lead him in the right direction and get more information than you ever expected. You could, for example, just start probing with no preliminaries.

"But you'd make a better impression if you said: 'Before I can be sure that my proposition makes sense for you, Mr. Greenfield, I need some details about your operation. Do you mind if I ask some questions?' "

The implication that his products must have real value for the prospect before he will press for the sale insures a respectful hearing for this salesman. He then follows up with his preplanned line of inquiry: "Have profits kept pace with volume?" "How do your operating expenses compare with others in your field?"

These and similar questions further the sale in two ways. First, they reinforce the feeling that this salesman will press for the sale only if the facts warrant it. Second, they help the prospect sell himself, for his every answer establishes in his own mind the potential value of the proposition.

LISTEN BEFORE YOU LEAP

Inquiry becomes an empty exercise unless you cultivate the art of *listening*. Charles B. Roth, in his book *Professional Salesmanship,* tells an illuminating story about Saunders Norvell, an outstanding sales executive.

Early in his selling career a bad sore throat forced Norvell to do a lot more listening than talking for a full week. Much to his surprise, he recorded more sales than in any previous week-long stretch. Experimenting further, Norvell talked more on some days, less on others. He consistently scored more on "listening days" than on "talking days."

"But," Norvell adds, "keeping quiet is not the point. You listen to find out what's bothering the prospect—then you *do something about it.*"

CHANGING IN MIDSTREAM

Sometimes what you suspect may be the chief selling point is not at all what interests the prospect most. But his response to your queries will usually put you on the right track—if you listen.

That's where inquiry pays off doubly. It not only predisposes your prospect to listen to you; it forces you to listen to him, and to shed your preconceived notion when indicated.

Here is a case in point, where the salesman thought he had dug out the basic selling point on his previous call. "Tom," said the salesman, "have you given any more thought to equipping your men with H-7 leak detectors?"

"No. In our type of business a half-ounce leak won't really hurt."

"Yes, I know that. But don't you have to check out all your jobs for leaks, big and small?"

(Here the inquiry was directing the prospect's attention to what the salesman thought was the main issue.)

"That's true. Still and all, $230 per machine is a lot of money when you need one for each crew."

(While the customer partly agreed, his answer made clear that the checkout was no real problem to him. But the query did bring out the real issue—the cost—which enabled the salesman to come to grips with it at once, with more inquiry.)

"Let's see. You told me your boys are having trouble finding the leaks on two of your installations. How much time have they already spent on them?"

"Thirty-one hours."

"Thirty-one hours? And what do you pay them now?" Here the salesman paused and let the prospect work over that thought in his mind.

After a couple of minutes of absolute silence, the prospect said: "I'll tell you what. Take your detectors over to those jobs. If you can find those leaks as fast as you claim, you can leave one leak detector with each crew. Call me for confirmation on those two and for two more."

The moral? Once you dig out the main selling point by really listening to your prospect's answers, you're well on your way to helping him sell himself.

Sometimes, of course, it takes a lot of experience to create a query right on the spot. But as this salesman points out, if you've prepared your main line of inquiry beforehand, "you're mentally geared to move wherever the customer takes you."

PLANT THE SEED OF DESIRE

Up to this point discussion has centered mainly on getting the information you need. But once you know the facts and have ideas about your approach, you may often want a soft-sell way of getting your points into the prospect's mind —a way of "planting the seed." Here again inquiry best serves the purpose.

A banker who was trying to cultivate a business account heard from a reliable source that the aging principals were somewhat worried about the continuation of the business. However, he did not want to reveal his knowledge, nor did he want to be too blunt in suggesting they do something to secure the firm's future.

His solution? He asked: "Have you ever considered how this business could be carried on if either partner were incapacitated?"

You might call this reverse inquiry. You know the facts; but you inquire so that the prospect can learn them painlessly or "inform" you under his own head of steam. At the same time, the query softly injects a promise.

Not that seed planting must be limited to potentially embarrassing situations. It can be used whenever a soft-sell approach seems indicated or when you want to imply that the prospect is missing out on something by not dealing with you and your firm.

For example, mutual funds salesman Phil Leeds reports that the following query works very well for him: "Mr. Garson, did you know that only a very small percentage of the people who own stocks do their own studying of the market?"

On the surface, this doesn't really say very much, though it seems to be imparting information. But the query does imply that the fund management can do a more effective job of studying the market than the prospect can do for himself. And it is precisely this implication that makes it a "seed planter."

TACKLE THE COMPETITION DIPLOMATICALLY

The same "reverse inquiry" touch is one of the best soft-sell ways of tackling competing lines. Instead of knocking the competition, which can often lose the prospect, you ask questions designed to help him draw his own conclusions, as illustrated by the following example.

How one man beat price competition

A prospect was shopping around for the best water treatment contract. When the salesman for Acme quoted his price, the prospect remarked: "I guess Empire [Acme's local competitor] was right when it said it was giving me the lowest possible quote."

This salesman knew that Empire underpriced him. He also knew that its price was based on a serious fault. But he was too canny a salesman to attack his competitor directly. Instead, he set the scene for the clincher with his first pointed query: "Are you considering dry or liquid scale remover?"

"Liquid is what Empire quoted me on."

"I see. Well, it's certainly true that liquid scale remover is faster and cheaper. But tell me, does Empire guarantee you against corroded metal parts?"

(Note how he freely admits the merits of the competing product before he slips in the question that alerts his prospect to a serious problem: corrosion.)

"Guarantee?" the prospect repeated. "Nothing was said about a guarantee. Do you offer one?"

"No. In fact, we don't use liquid removers at all because they're a bit tricky to handle. They produce heavy fumes as soon as you open the container, which can be dangerous if there is no air circulating. And those fumes will corrode metal parts. That's why we recommend powdered removers. They are safer to handle, and they contain more effective inhibitors for the best protection of metals."

Of course, that salesman knew that his competitor could not possibly guarantee the safety of the highly unpredictable liquid remover. To say so directly, however, would only touch off the "he's just knocking the competition" reaction. Instead, he planted the information in the form of a question. He could be sure of the answer only because he had acquired sound knowledge of his competition.

Inquiry opens the door

When the competition is already entrenched, there's always the danger of raising the prospect's hackles by implying that he made a mistake in judgment when he bought the other brand. Each salesman for the leading firm in the highly competitive paper towel field is trained to avoid this danger by using inquiry. When he calls on a prospect, he opens with something like this:

"Mr. Johnson, would you like to cut down on an expense item that piles up every day—and that adds up to a much higher sum than need be spent?"

(This plants a seed of dissatisfaction: that the prospect is losing money he shouldn't be losing. Naturally, most prospects agree that they would like to cut unnecessary costs.)

"Have you ever been in a washroom and seen a man pull out two, four, or even six towels while drying his hands and face?"

"Sure."

"Do you think this happens in your washrooms?"

"I know it does."

(The salesman knows it too. But he uses reverse inquiry to let the prospect "inform" him of this key fact, which raises a doubt about the quality of the competing brand.)

Pulling a paper towel out of his pocket, the salesman asks: "Does this look different from any other paper towel?"

"No."

"But it has a built-in feature which makes it unnecessary to use more than one towel to dry face and hands thoroughly and thus cuts out a large share of waste. May I show you how it works?"

"I'll take a look."

Without making a direct reference to the competing line, the salesman paves the way to a demonstration of quality solely through inquiry. Not that this leads to an order every time, but enough orders come in to keep this firm well ahead of its field.

Help the Prospect Sell Himself

Plenty of people just don't like to be told. No matter how much they stand to gain, if you tell them flatly "I think you ought to try . . . ," you may well lose them. And some won't listen because they don't like your outfit.

In such cases a broad question of opinion which invites the prospect to talk may work when nothing else will.

Here is an amusing case in point. Many years ago, when William Wrigley started his career as a soap salesman, he stumbled onto the value of this technique. In all innocence he walked into a store and asked for an order, only to find that the proprietor hated the firm Wrigley represented.

"You and your company can go to hell!" the grocer snarled.

Young Wrigley started to close his kit. "I guess there's no point trying to sell you," he said mildly. "But I'm a new salesman and I wonder if you might give me some pointers. What could I say to other prospects in order to make more sales?"

"My lad," the grocer began—and went into a detailed lecture on how to sell the very soaps he had turned down. You guessed it: he made such a good job of it that he sold himself.

That's how young Wrigley learned a very important lesson. The man you can't sell may sell himself—if you give him a chance to talk.

Most people love the sound of their own voices. Ask their advice, as Wrigley did, and the dam will frequently burst. Not that the prospect must launch into a speech; he can sell himself with just one or two remarks, as the next case aptly illustrates.

Selling a $10 shaving brush

Jack Willis used to be a divisional sales manager for a drug wholesaler. Some years ago the firm took on a line of high-quality shaving brushes, retailing from $10 up.

Jack gave his men a pep talk about the profit margins they'd earn for the dealer and distributor alike; then he stressed the fat commissions for the salesmen.

But it left the men cold. With electric shavers and brushless creams, who would buy shaving brushes for $10 and more?"

In the field some of the salesmen went through the motions. "By the way, can you use some badger shaving brushes?"

"What are they worth?"

"They sell from $10 up."

"Ten dollars for shaving brushes? Nobody spends that kind of money on a shaving brush."

"Well, do you want to look at them?"

"Stop wasting my time."

When spending a day in the field with some of his men, Jack bet two of them that he could sell the brushes in certain stores. Here's how he won his bet.

When the right time came, he'd say to a selected dealer: "You've got a nice shop here. I guess you must get your share of high-class customers, people with money who like good things."

(Planting the idea that this was a luxury market.)

Out of pride, if for no other reason, the dealer would say: "Oh, yes, I attract some quality customers. There's a banker [or a big lawyer or whatever was true in that case] who comes in here once in a while, and a few others like him."

"Do you think they might buy some real top-quality products for personal use with money no object?"

"I guess some might at that."

"Well, if they found a line of high-class toilet goods here, do you think they might come back more often for other quality items, the kind that give you a bigger profit margin?"

(Planting the seed of desire: bigger margins.)

"You've got a point there; it certainly sounds logical."

"If you got some good promotional help, do you think you might sell these items as gifts for people for whom it is hard to buy?"

"That could be; it could work, especially at Christmas."

(With his last two remarks, the dealer was selling himself.)

"As long as you feel that way about it, I want to show you our line of shaving brushes, every one of them made exclusively from genuine badger bristles. They sell for as low as $10 each, and up to $150 for the larger brushes, which have only the rare silver-tipped badger bristles. They're wonderful gift items—especially for older men who have everything. We sell them only to people who care about quality and who can and are willing to pay for it."

"Let me see what they look like."

And Jack made the sale. Now let's analyze how he did it.

1. With his opening comment and questions, Jack appealed to curiosity and desire for gain—and thus aroused interest.

2. All his questions were you-minded—directed at what the prospect thought this would do for him, and so on. Thus Jack displayed concern for his prospect's needs.

3. He let the selling idea—the building of a quality gift trade—become the dealer's idea. Once the prospect added on his own "especially at Christmas," Jack knew the idea had taken hold.
4. He immediately drove home the "this is your idea" approach quite neatly with his "As long as you feel that way about it. . . ."

Any way you look at it, this was a masterly job of inquiry and selling.

He lets his prospects help him ask

In a variation of this technique Stan Leggett, who sells intangible "problem solvers," cleverly combines skillful inquiry with the dramatic pause. Initially Stan lets his prospects fan their interest in his product with their own questions. When he finally takes over to focus on their specific problems, they have half sold themselves. His inquiry helps them complete the job.

This creative inquiry—prepared well before his call—has made Stan his firm's top producer. Here is a typical example of Stan at work.

"Mr. Grimes, I'm Stanley Leggett. I represent the Cinelab Industrial Communications Associates."

Pause. "Oh, does your company make films?"

"In a way; but that's not our real job."

"What do you do then?"

"We solve problems."

Pause. "Do you mean you can solve some of our problems with your films?"

With this expression of interest Stan makes a quick switch and takes over the questioning.

"That depends on the kind of problems you have. Tell me, Mr. Grimes, is your main problem with labor, manufacturing, or selling?"

(Here he starts getting close to the prospect's problem while implying: "I won't talk films unless you have the kind of problem we can help solve.")

"Right now I'd say we have mostly a selling problem."

"Does it lie in getting your salesmen to know the product better or in educating your distributors to do a better merchandising job?"

"I think they could both stand to know a lot more."

And so it goes. By the time Stan finishes his queries he has the prospect telling him exactly the kind of communications film he needs. Making the sale is the logical outcome.

Building the Habit

Inquiry is the key to your prospect's needs and interests. In planning your line of inquiry for each call, consider the the following points:

1. Do you have a good door-opening query? If not, work one out right then and there.
2. Do you know what selling points will most appeal to the prospect or customer? If not, prepare a line of inquiry designed to dig out this information tactfully.
3. Have you prepared a few dramatic queries that might plant the seed of a sale?
4. If you're working against tough competition, can you advantageously use soft-sell inquiry and reverse inquiry to tip the balance in your favor? If so, develop your questions in advance.

5. Can you work out a line of inquiry that will help the prospect talk himself into the sale?

After each call, review the interview mentally. Did you take every opportunity to use the soft-sell tone imparted by thoughtful inquiry? Did you use inquiry sufficiently to uncover the needs of your prospect or customer? If your answers to such self-examination are on the negative side, develop a plan to improve your application of inquiry for your next contact.

6

Benefits:

The Key to Buying Decisions

Here we see how the O PIB'ROC principles mesh. When you adopt a specific, constructive objective for each call, when you prepare for the call by analyzing your prospect's needs, when you inquire to dig out his interests, you're automatically getting you-minded—putting yourself on his side of the fence.

And that's the best of all approaches. To make the most of each fundamental principle, you have to think and talk about the buyer's wants and needs. All of which takes you well on your way toward talking benefits. And it's talking benefits that moves the sale along toward the close.

How benefits and the you-minded attitude hang together will become increasingly clear as we focus on four major areas:

Sell the benefit, not the product.
Sell the benefit the prospect wants.
Sell the differences.
Drive the benefits home.

SELL THE BENEFIT, NOT THE PRODUCT

What is the key to more and better sales? Every salesman knows the answer.

"Sell the benefits!" they will tell you. Yet it costs us
money every day in needlessly lost sales because we don't
practice what we know.

Why do experienced salesmen sometimes miss the boat?
Because, strangely enough, they're so absorbed in their
products—as all good salesmen are. For unless you think
through your presentation carefully, it's all too easy to confuse technical descriptions with benefits.

"Mister, will it keep me warm?"

Consider the classic story of the salesman who set out to
sell a heating unit to an elderly lady. He waxed enthusiastic
about the construction features, talked about BTUs, thermo-
stats, and automatic damper controls.

Then, when he paused for breath, the little old lady
came up with this wonderfully human question: "Tell me,
mister, will it keep me warm?"

THE BENEFIT TWINS

Being human, a buyer is motivated by self-interest.
Which means that you'll more surely attract his attention

when you touch on the one matter that truly fascinates him: "What's in it for me?"

And that's precisely the point of that old story. To put it bluntly, your prospect doesn't give a hoot about your goods or services, but he'd sure like to know what they can do for him.

Generally speaking, your product or service can save time, money, labor, and the like. Or it can give more production, profits, efficiency, safety, and so on. Organize your thinking and talking around these benefit twins—*saving* and *giving*—and you're bound to hit squarely on the benefits target far more often.

When you say, for example, "This alloy covers steel with a film of chromium oxide," you're being a vanadium technician.

But suppose you translate that into "By shielding steel from water vapor, salt, and sulfur, this alloy gives you corrosion-resistant stainless steel—which will double the life of equipment operating under conditions similar to yours."

Then you're being a vanadium salesman.

It's a matter of viewpoint

To make the point clear, let us take a more subtle example, a case in which the salesman thought he was selling the benefit until he stopped to think it through.

"Not long ago," this representative writes, "when I started pushing our new line of trucks, I called on a small, well-managed transportation firm. The company had a good following, but it was losing some business to larger competitors that could give faster pick-up service.

"By describing our heavy-duty bearings with all the enthusiasm I felt for them, I got across the point that here was a motor which wouldn't choke up under the heaviest load. But my prospect turned me down.

"Yet I knew this was a good item for him. Thinking it over, I saw where I had gone wrong. I had been talking from our point of view, describing what a wonderful motor we had developed. From his viewpoint, however, only one thing mattered: making more pick-ups with a given amount of equipment.

"So I went right back and told the prospect that there was one more question I wanted to ask: 'Would you like me to show you how our new trucks will help you get more freight?'

"That got his attention. And when I gave him evidence that our new motor had cut garaging time by 23 percent for another transportation firm, thus keeping more trucks on duty longer, I was well on my way toward the sale."

It's a matter of habit

Selling the benefits is not as simple as it may appear on the surface. That's because most salesmen *believe* they do it quite consistently. However, as a number of surveys on this subject have shown, salesmen all too often fail to take advantage of this powerful principle of selling.

For example, Porter Henry, Jr., one of the best-known marketing consultants in this country, tells how he made 78 calls with salesmen of a building supply company. In only two of these calls did the salesmen talk about what the goods or services would do for the dealer—the benefits. Sure, the salesmen spoke of the merits of the products they were selling; they took stock; they described promotional activities. But only twice did they apply the benefits principle. They had never made a habit of it.

Just remember the tagline "Mister, will it keep me warm?" and you'll be telling more and more of your prospects how your wares can help them save or gain. And that's all I mean when I say "Sell the benefits, not the product."

Sell the Benefit the Prospect Wants

Not all benefits are of equal value to every prospect. One man buys price; another, guaranteed supply; a third, quality or convenient service; a fourth, rapid turnover.

The moral? Simply this: the benefit which is of no interest to the man in front of you is *no benefit for that sale.*

Actually, many benefits have potential value for clinching a sale. It's all a matter of degree; to win a given prospect's full attention, you must first concentrate on the one benefit that matters most to him.

How can you tell? Here again we see how the basic principles of selling mesh. You can prepare beforehand; you can inquire at the point of sale.

Above all, you must be flexible. Drop *your* idea of what's most important when *his* reactions indicate otherwise. One example should underscore the point.

He was selling investment counsel...

"One morning," writes securities salesman Ralph Jenkins, "we received a postcard request to be put on the mailing list for our investment newsletter. Since this indicated the writer was a good prospect for our investment services, I phoned the customer at his office and told him I was pleased to put him on our mailing list.

" 'Are you in the market regularly?' I asked.

" 'Oh, yes!'

" 'Would you be interested in experienced and unbiased investment advice? Many of our customers feel we have helped them improve their holdings.' "

(The salesman presents what he assumes is a powerful benefit.)

" 'Frankly, I've been doing pretty well these past few years on my own,' the customer replied."

(If you were too intent on what you considered important, you might miss your cue here: that investment advice was not this man's primary concern. But in this case salesman Jenkins wisely shifted gears.)

... when the prospect wanted a time saver

"Quickly I dropped the 'investment counsel' gambit. It evidently did not appeal to this man. To gain time for hitting on some other selling point, I asked if he wanted to receive our mailings at his home or if he preferred to look them over in the office.

" 'I never have a spare minute in the office,' he said. 'I'd appreciate getting the newsletter at home.'

"This sounded promising. So I asked: 'How come you're so busy?'

"It turned out that the molded rubber fabricating plant which he owned had been steadily expanding. Keeping up with the orders took every minute of his time.

" 'It certainly sounds like a dynamic business,' I said. 'Since your time is so valuable, have you ever considered how an investment account could take some of the time-consuming chores off your back?'

" 'Like what?'

" 'We can probably save you more than a week of your

time each year just by more thorough and efficient handling of your maturing investments. Would you like to meet me at lunch sometime next week so we can discuss it further?'

"Obviously, I had now hit upon the right benefit, because he made an appointment for the following Monday. The upshot was that he opened an investment management account to the tune of $400,000."

SELLING IN DEPTH

In the field of industrial goods it is often necessary to convince a number of executives, engineers, and supervisory officials before a sale can be closed. When negotiating such a sale, you must slant your product story in a different way for each man you see.

As one salesman says: "I used to give our whole story to everyone I saw. But now that I tailor my approach to the specific man I'm dealing with, I *take less time* and *maintain more interest* at every level of negotiation.

"For example, we put out a plastic container which is 15 times lighter than glass ones formerly used. I find I get more mileage from my calls by converting that general benefit—low weight—into different specific benefits.

"Shop men think of the reduced weight in terms of easier handling. Purchasing agents translate the lower weight into reduced shipping costs. Because it reduces fatigue, management sees the benefit in terms of increased efficiency and production. The impact on each man is sharper when I emphasize that part of the story which most interests him."

That's it in a nutshell. Every man you must see—from the purchasing agent to the president—has his own areas of interest. In each case you must shape your story accordingly.

BACKDOOR SELLING

Over and over again, experience has shown that the industrial representative gets many of his best leads in the customer's plant. Which brings up the problem of "backdoor selling."

Salesmen sometimes complain: "I can't get past the purchasing agent." Buyers in turn understandably dislike the salesman who bypasses them and calls on others in the firm without referral. One survey found that this procedure prejudiced some 75 percent of the purchasing agents queried. About 60 percent of the firms surveyed had rules against it; 95 percent made provisions for salesmen to contact other personnel through the purchasing office.

The pros and cons. The merits of the case can be endlessly debated. Indeed, the subject was discussed at the Sales Executives Club of New York. Here is part of that debate.

"When a purchasing agent won't let you present your case to a man who can evaluate it adequately," said M. J. Hoover, vice president of sales of the Sun Chemical Corporation, "you may have to find a back door."

"If you feel you must go around the purchasing agent, maybe you haven't done a good job of selling him," said David S. Gibson, purchasing vice president of Worthington Corporation, in rebuttal.

Sometimes, Mr. Gibson conceded, if the buyer doesn't know his job or is jealous of his authority, "tact and ingenuity are needed to obtain permission to call on others. But if the buyer doesn't have the technical knowledge to see the value of your product, try to educate him first. He'll appreciate it. For it will make him look good if he can add some knowledgeable comment to his referral."

If you must, you must...

As a rule, the salesman should avoid backdoor selling. After all, the buyer is on the customer's side of the fence, and there's no point offending him. But if you must, you must.

For example, workers in one chemical plant had to loosen the electrode clamps on a phosphate furnace six times every 24 hours; using wrenches, three or four men could complete the operation in about 12 minutes. Although salesman Henry Baxter had an air-powered tool which enabled one man to do the job in 3 minutes, he couldn't get past the buyer, who, Henry says, "obviously favored a competing supplier."

Well, one day Henry just walked into that plant on his own. It took one quick demonstration of benefits to get a requisition sent in. Through savings in power, labor, and down time, the tool paid for itself in three months.

. . . but give him the credit

Though it is wise to avoid backdoor selling, when you feel you must emulate Henry, remember Mr. Hoover's final admonition: "If you are forced to 'backdoor' to get your order, it is still good practice to give the buyer as much credit as possible and to let him know you appreciate whatever cooperation he gives you."

He got the sales manager on his side

To sell in depth effectively, you should consider calling on any man who might help you. If you can show that your product will boost your prospect's sales, even sales management might lend a hand, as happened in this case.

A salesman of paint-spraying equipment sought an order from a household appliance manufacturer. Having visited the plant, he knew that the firm could well improve its layout and enameling equipment. But he made little progress with the assistant works manager.

Convinced that the poor enameling had an adverse effect on sales, the representative made an appointment to see the general sales manager. After some discussion, the sales manager admitted that some customers had complained that the enamel started to chip during the first year of use.

That was the opening the salesman was waiting for. "We've helped our customers lick that sort of problem before. You see, we don't sell standardized equipment. We design enameling layouts and spray-booth equipment to fit your individual specifications."

Then and there the sales manager picked up the phone and arranged for a meeting with the works manager and a couple of engineers. After two intensive discussions, a requisition was sent in for the salesman's equipment.

Always ask yourself: "Who in this firm should know about my product?" "What benefits angle will appeal most to him?" Figure out your answers before you make your appointment. Then slant your story in that direction.

Sell the Differences

What do you do when you want to remove your offer from competitive comparisons? Every salesman knows the answer: *emphasize the differences.*

Single out the one benefit unique to your product or organization.

"We're the only firm that stands behind a blender with

an unconditional two-year guarantee." "Our tape is tougher because it's made of Krafft paper." And so on.

The principle is simple enough—and sound. The trouble is, it doesn't always work out that easily, for every salesman is looking for the same differences. And as many salesmen have complained upon occasion: "There's no benefit I can offer that can't be matched by one or another of my competitors."

This does create a problem. Often the issue may turn on personalized contacts: the salesman who makes friends more easily or who has an introduction from the right person may well get the jump on his competitors.

But it's much sounder to build on the basis of differences *you create*. The extra benefit that only you dream up will be unique to you and your institution. While a winning personality doesn't hurt, in the long run it's the extra benefit that makes more friends and influences more people.

How do you do it? You can create important differences in two ways: (1) remove your story from competitive comparisons, (2) remember you're part of the package.

REMOVE YOUR STORY FROM COMPETITIVE
COMPARISONS

Sometimes you have a corner on a particular benefit, even if it is only short-lived. If, for example, yours is the only firm that offers a wide choice of colors, you'll play that benefit for all it's worth, as long as the monopoly lasts.

But I am concerned with a more subtle procedure. That is, you and your competition are offering essentially the same advantages, but you fashion a unique difference for yourself by being the only one to package a particular feature as a benefit. An example will show what I mean.

He created a "monopoly"

Here's how one salesman did it. He had a request for a quote on equipment for a $-2°$ walk-in cooler. He planned a quality job: air-cooled equipment with hot-gas defrost.

Aware that his quote would probably place him in a higher bidding bracket than his competition, he followed a two-point formula which had worked for him in similar cases. (1) He prepared a strategy that created a "monopoly" situation, giving him a benefit that was unique for that sale. (2) Instead of attacking the competition, he let a well-planned series of questions help the prospect reach the conclusion that the proposal was right for him and his customer. Here, in capsule form, is how the actual interview went.

When the salesman presented his quotation, the prospect said: "You are $2,200 higher than my other bidder, though he is quoting on water-cooled equipment."

"Have you thought of the advantages for your customer of air-cooled equipment coupled with hot-gas defrost?" the salesman countered.

"No," the prospect admitted.

The salesman had thoroughly prepared himself. He took this opportunity to present the benefits one at a time and to get full acceptance from his prospect on each point. Then he asked: "Do you think your customer would find such an installation preferable?"

"I'm sure he would, but not for $2,200 extra. Price means a lot to him."

Having made his first point—that the installation he proposed was in a truly different category—the salesman intensified his presentation with another "monopoly" difference. He asked: "Has your other bidder quoted on a tower and circulation pump to prevent wasting water?"

The contractor looked up the bid. There was no such provision.

(The salesman had sensed that the lower quote did not include this extra equipment. With his pointed query, he alerted the prospect while avoiding a direct attack upon his competitor.)

After showing the prospect that a tower and pump quote would make the two bids more competitive, he pressed the point home by asking: "Will your price-conscious customer stand for the cost of chemical treatments and for the water bills he'll get with that installation wasting 1,800 gallons per hour?"

"You've got a good point there," said the contractor. "But I have already given my customer a rough quote, and I doubt that he'll pay any more."

At this stage the contractor had clearly accepted the point that the air-cooled equipment would serve the purpose better. There now remained the problem of getting the contractor's customer to accept the higher-quality installation.

The representative tackled this with another prepared query: "If your customer could take a quick look at an installation very similar to the one I propose and see exactly how much he could save on his operating costs, do you think he might consider a larger initial investment?"

(Here again, this excellent salesman avoided the skepticism that might accompany a flat statement. Instead, he brought out his point by the question he had carefully framed before the interview: the question suggesting the examination of an installation.)

"I think that would be a good idea," said the contractor.

"Fine. I've got a user nearby who is very pleased with this type of equipment. He'll be happy to let your customer see how it works."

The appointment was made and ultimately the sale went through. "It doesn't work every time," this salesman points out, "but I've been landing a gratifying number of high-bid sales following this 'monopoly benefit' approach."

The point you bring out counts

The representative of a structural steel firm creates a competitive edge for himself by stressing "personalized service" in every proposal. "We have won a well-deserved reputation for delivering in exact accord with your needs," he tells his prospects. "Our office maintains daily contact, if you wish. This plan conserves your limited storage space, yet it insures against holding up your high-priced labor for lack of material."

His competitors offer the same service. *But nothing is truly a benefit until someone sells it as such.* If only you play it up, only you will reap the harvest from it.

Once you think about it in those terms, you can almost always find some point you can develop into a difference only because your competitors ignore it as too small or routine. For example:

> You can give better or faster service.
> You can make ordering simpler.
> You can get quotations faster.
> You can bring in display and promotion ideas.
> You can suggest new applications.

REMEMBER YOU'RE PART OF THE PACKAGE

Salesmen often forget that one of the biggest benefits they can offer is the value of their own constructive thinking and services. When you need that extra benefit to clinch a deal, just remember: you're part of the package. Your personal service and ideas or your intimate knowledge of the product and its applications might well be the difference— the extra benefit that pulls in the extra business.

This might be as simple as personal follow-through on delivery promises. Or when the size of the sale so warrants, it might involve more elaborate preparation, as illustrated by the following example.

In this case, fittingly enough, a crack salesman for a financing corporation used the very idea of sales training to create a constructive difference which helped him beat the strong competition offered by a local bank. Both the bank and the finance company were out to discount the prospect's paper. Whichever firm he signed with, that dealer would enjoy the usual benefits: improved cash flow, prompt service, and so on.

From his previous visits to the prospect's showrooms, the salesman knew that the dealer's time sales had been slipping somewhat over the past few years. But he was sure that the trend could be reversed if sales personnel were adequately trained in the selling of time-payment contracts. Stressing this, he felt, would give him the crucial difference that might make his package stand out.

At a luncheon meeting with the customer the salesman outlined his idea of a training program to help the sales force sell "add on" purchases. He showed how sales personnel could be helped to introduce the subject of installment buying more successfully; how they could learn to do an even better job of servicing their more difficult customers; and how this improved salesmanship might well build application volume.

Taken with this idea, the customer followed through with a training program conducted by his sales manager.

Result? The dealer's sales improved—and last year the salesman's firm purchased more than $600,000 of his paper.

There's no doubt about it. The constructive approach you dream up is truly unique. Through it you create specific differences which no competitor can offer.

DRIVE THE BENEFITS HOME

Since selling the benefits is perhaps the most universally acknowledged sales principle, your prospects and customers will be getting a steady diet of benefits from your competitors as well as from you. This creates a certain amount of skepticism which makes the most outstanding benefit just a claim until your prospect accepts it as true.

That's why you'll give yourself an edge if you take your benefits story one step further. That is, convert each point from unsubstantiated claim to living reality. You can do this most effectively in five ways:

Use figures.
Cite examples.
Call on a third-party witness.
Make comparisons.
Use demonstrations.

USE FIGURES

Having traveled with well over a thousand salesmen representing a wide variety of products and services, I can testify to the many, many occasions when specific figures transformed a dubious-sounding claim to an accepted benefit. Consider, for example, the truck salesman referred to earlier who was met with open skepticism by his prospect.

Yet he made the sale when he drove the benefit home with figures: the valid evidence that his new motor had cut garaging time for another transportation firm by 23 percent.

CITE EXAMPLES

All great teachers have made wide use of examples to communicate more effectively. Throughout this book, I too have employed this valuable teaching device. No sooner is a generalized claim made than it is illustrated with a case history.

You can use exactly the same method to convert a benefit from a claim to a reality. All you need is a good case or two for each of your selling points.

One salesman was selling the benefit of his firm's sound claims policy to a dealer who was having trouble with a present supplier. "Our company," said the salesman, "has a long-standing policy: we handle all claims promptly and to the customer's satisfaction. Just a short time ago, *for example,* a claim developed over a damaged shipment. The buyer called us for help in getting an adjustment. We had a man on the job within a few hours and handled everything for him. Maybe you would like to talk with the customer on the telephone? I'll put the call through on my credit card.

"Of course, we don't like to have claims. But we like even less to have a dissatisfied customer."

This example satisfied the dealer. He wouldn't even let the salesman put the call through.

CALL ON A THIRD-PARTY WITNESS

Had the prospect in the previous case remained skeptical, talking with the customer whose claim had been so well handled would no doubt have convinced him that the representative's presentation of his company's adjustments policy as a benefit was entirely justified.

Using a third-party witness is akin to citing an example —but more powerful. The salesman presenting a benefit is a prejudiced party. The third-party witness has no stake in making the sale. Moreover, his prestige or the nature of his job may add weight to what he says.

As with all the other techniques discussed here, much greater use could be made of third-party witnesses. Most satisfied customers like to tell of their experience. Just one caution: make sure you've got their approval.

MAKE COMPARISONS

Before most sales are consummated, buyers make their own comparisons. Why not help them, thereby validating your claimed benefits at the same time?

"I was endeavoring to sell an account reconciliation plan to a customer," a banker said. "While agreeing that it probably was a good idea, he did not become interested *until we actually compared the time required for his present plan with that of the proposed plan.* As a result, he agreed to this service. His account reconciliations are now completed in less than 5 hours instead of between 30 and 35 hours. He has been able to eliminate one employee without disrupting his internal procedure."

USE DEMONSTRATIONS

Demonstrations are dramatic and powerful devices for punching home the benefits of products and services. They could be used far more frequently than they are—and to greater advantage. Nor do they need to be elaborate; just a touch of imagination will often do.

For example, building materials salesmen are often asked if this or that material will take a nail well. Most will say yes and leave it at that. One man commands more attention—and action—with a simple demonstration of his own devising. After getting a sample of the material from his car along with a hammer and some nails, he says: "Try it for yourself."

In so doing, customers drive home the benefit to themselves.

BUILDING THE HABIT

Before each contact, prepare your benefits story. You may find it helpful to use the following procedure:

1. On the left-hand side of a sheet of paper, put down every selling point you want to get across to your prospect or customer. (Prior preparation or inquiry will have told you.)
2. On the right side of the page, translate each point into a benefit—that is, what it will save or gain for the prospect.
3. Choose the most attention-catching opening promise: the right benefit for that specific prospect.
4. Work out something as an "extra" or difference in case of competition.
5. Consider the benefits of your own thinking or service.
6. Choose the best way to drive each major benefit home.

After each call, review the interview mentally. If it didn't go as well as it should have, think back carefully.

Did you leave out any benefit that might have helped? Did you spell out clearly enough those you used? Are you sure you presented your product in terms of what it would do for the prospect—rather than describing how it works?

From your answers to these questions you will know what changes, if any, are needed to make your benefits story crystal clear to your next prospect.

7

Wrap-up:

The Key to Winning Acceptance
Step by Step

Sometimes salesmen make the mistake of assuming that a prospect has absorbed and accepted each benefit they present because he nods and says yes. Ask for the order, however, and the yes can quickly change to no.

Why? Because no matter how alert he may be, a buyer will at times get only a limited impression of your story the first time around, especially if your proposition is new or somewhat technical. But often he will nod in agreement because he doesn't like to say that he has not fully understood your points, or because he'd like to get rid of you faster.

Obviously, spelling out a benefit will have little effect in clinching a sale unless your prospect understands and accepts it. Yet as various point-of-sale studies reveal, many representatives go through their presentations without stopping to see if their benefits register—a practice which loses many a sale that might otherwise be made.

That's where wrap-up comes in. To make sure your benefits are really getting across, you should follow a two-step procedure. (1) Focus the prospect's attention on but one major benefit at a time. (2) Taking nothing for granted, test his understanding and acceptance of that major benefit *before you proceed to the next.* If his answer shows he has fully grasped the point and agrees with it, move on to the next one. Otherwise, backtrack: repeat the benefit in different words and check him out on it again.

Simple, isn't it? Yet experience shows that salesmen do a better job if they work out their wrap-up approach beforehand.

PREPARING YOUR WRAP-UP STRATEGY

No matter how simple or complex your story, when you tell it the wrap-up way you get it across more quickly, more clearly, and more compellingly. But don't count on pulling good qualifying queries out of your hat; prepare them before the interview. Of course, you must be flexible; you should be able to make on-the-spot changes when the prospect's responses suggest it.

CONSIDER EVERY MAJOR BENEFIT

In applying the benefits principle, you have already noted each point you want to make and how you will put it across. Not that you'll relentlessly plod your way through your entire armory of benefits at every interview. Often you'll have some idea of the prospect's interests before the interview, and you'll mold your story accordingly.

Even when you have no line on your prospect, you'll usually pick up a clue as the interview progresses. And with your benefits brief at your fingertips, you won't be caught flat-footed.

Generally you should present your entire benefits story to note what seems most significant to him. In a few instances you may zero in on one benefit today and give a second the full treatment tomorrow. But when you have the full range of benefits to choose from, you are in the most favorable position to clinch the sale.

WORK OUT A LOGICAL SEQUENCE

With salesmen's permission, research men have used tape recorders to find out what happens in real-life sales contacts. In most cases representatives start with one point, go on to a second or third without pausing to gain acceptance, return to the first or second point, jump to the fourth, and so on—making it difficult for the prospect to follow the thread of the story and for the salesman to know which points, if any, have been grasped and accepted.

When you pitch into your presentation without knowing where your prospect stands from one moment to the next, it's easy to confuse him. And you'll often lose him completely if you barge ahead while his mind dwells on a point he has not fully understood or agreed with.

True, a spontaneous approach sparks enthusiasm in seller and prospect alike. But *a planned story need not be a canned one.* With your benefits arranged in well-plotted sequence, you're always on top of the situation, leaving yourself free to tell your story in your own freshly minted words and to change the sequence as desirable.

When your benefits story is well planned, interruptions rarely throw you off. Despite phone calls and people popping in and out, you can readily pick up the thread of the story with no loss of time or equilibrium. What's more, your presentation flows with a cumulative impact that often makes buying the only logical conclusion.

When planning your sequence, give special attention to your opening and closing shots. Your opening benefit should be powerful enough to gain your prospect's undivided attention. Your closing point should set him up for the sale.

Let me clear up what is often a major misunderstanding. "Wrap-up" as used here does not mean gaining the account (though it will often do so). That's the principle of closing. In this context "wrap-up" means only one thing: making sure your prospect understands and accepts each major point and, if he doesn't, going back to it for another try.

PREPARE CONFIRMING (QUALIFYING) QUESTIONS

When you tie each point in your proposal to the prospect's needs, when he understands what it's designed to do for him, and when he agrees that it will do it, you're well on your way to the account. But remember: *you can't take understanding and acceptance for granted just because he's nodding his head.*

You've got to reach for it actively. How?

Mostly by asking, by slanting each question directly at the point of issue. As long as any doubt remains in the prospect's mind, the atmosphere will be unpropitious for closing. Probing for confirmation of benefits with wrap-up queries is one of the best ways of smoking out still unvoiced resistance, thereby giving yourself another chance to drive the benefit home.

"Do you see how this plan will increase your store traffic?" A negative response to such a confirming query gives you a chance to strengthen your selling foundation. Conversely, every positive response tells you that you can move on to the next point; at the same time, it puts the prospect in a buying frame of mind.

MIX YOUR QUESTIONS UP

In applying the wrap-up principle, you sometimes reach out for a simple yes-or-no answer, as in the above case. At other times you want to avoid such a limited response. For if you fall into a set pattern, your prospect may start "yessing" you automatically, even when he doesn't understand the point.

Besides, reaching for a yes too often inevitably leaves a hard-sell impression. Ask your prospect once or even twice "Do you agree?" and his yes may come freely enough. Ask him a third or fourth time, however, and he may feel that you are trying to pressure him into acceptance.

It's much better to give him the facts and then to ask the kind of wrap-up question that will cause him to think the situation out, applying your proposal mentally to his own conditions. A positive response will then be meaningful. So mix your questions up.

"How much of a market do you think there is for a toothpaste designed specifically for smokers—to whiten their teeth?" "What effect would such a promotion have on your frozen food volume?" "Approximately how much labor do you think this procedure will eliminate?"

Such questions require more than a simple yes or no. When your prospect starts thinking along these lines, he becomes involved—he begins translating the plan into very real benefits for himself. Thus his reply gives you a better indication of where you stand.

When acceptance is confirmed, you can move on to the next point in full confidence that your prospect is with you. When his answers reveal lack of understanding or agreement, repeat the benefit in different words—then reach for agreement again.

How one salesman did it

A chemicals manufacturer, which I will call Chemcorp, sells polyplastilene powder to plastic molders. Its representatives operate in a highly competitive market where every producer puts out virtually the same product.

One salesman was trying to get his firm accepted as a second source of supply by one of the larger plastic molders, which bought the powder in carload lots. Achieving his goal in the face of a solidly entrenched competitor took a lot of selling. Let's look over the shoulder of that Chemcorp salesman and see how he did it.

This man had seven benefits to work with: company reliability, guaranteed supply, elimination of storage problems, minimization of inventory, fast delivery, reliable service, and a multiple source of supply.

Tackling these benefits in the sequence his experience dictated, the salesman divided some sheets of paper down the middle for noting point by point the benefits, proofs, and wrap-up queries. His chart looked like this:

BENEFITS	QUALIFYING QUERIES
Chemcorp Reliability	
1. Testing program. Our record: customer satisfaction.	1. Have I given sufficient evidence to assure you that we can provide a uniform product?
2. Close cooperation with customer.	2. How do you feel about it?
Guaranteed Supply	
1. We lease a fleet of boxcars specially equipped for shipping polyplastilene; maintain a car on your siding; replace when empty.	1. How would our plan affect your supply needs?
2. Demurrage waived.	2. Others have told us that waiving the demurrage charges makes our plan even more attractive. Would that be of considerable advantage to you at times?

And so on for the other five benefits. Note that the proofs for each benefit are broken down into two parts. That helps eliminate repetition if your prospect does not accept a given benefit at once. You add point 2 the second time around, as well as repeating point 1 in different words.

For the same reason the salesman lists two qualifying queries: one for the first time, the other for backtracking when repetition is necessary and the prospect should be qualified again. When you have only two or three major benefits to put across, your preparation will be that much simpler. But whether you have few selling points or many, better organization wedded to carefully prepared wrap-up queries means more sales.

Now let us see how this prepared story was actually presented at the point of sale. First the salesman took up the question of Chemcorp's reliability. After concentrating on that one point for a time, he wound up by saying: "I think our reputation shows that we can guarantee the uniformity of every carload of polyplastilene we produce."

"That's what they all say," the prospect replied. "Every producer guarantees uniformity."

(In the face of this inadequate acceptance, the representative correctly refrained from going on to the next point. Instead, he backtracked, this time emphasizing the point in terms of close cooperation with the customer, just as he had planned to do if a second query proved necessary.)

"That's true," he replied. "But we specialize in working very closely with our customers to meet their particular requirements. That's why our chemists take time to match our customers' specifications precisely: in color, flowability, clarity, and particle size."

Then, after citing two examples illustrating the detailed steps his company had taken, he tried his second qualifying query: "Wouldn't you say that we provide an unusual degree of cooperation in meeting customers' specifications?" When the answer showed that the prospect now understood the point, the salesman dropped it and did not return to it until he made his final summary of the benefits he was offering.

Moving on to the second benefit, the salesman discussed the advantages of maintaining one of Chemcorp's constantly refilled boxcars on the prospect's own siding. When the prospect broke in to qualify himself with a remark about how the boxcar would ease the firm's storage problems, the salesman moved on again, with no further effort to elaborate the point.

(Here we see how the qualifying technique keeps you closely attuned to the prospect's wavelength. The first time the salesman would have lost the prospect had he not elaborated on the point. The second time he could have lost him had he insisted on pressing the point after the prospect qualified himself. There's nothing duller than listening to repetitive arguments for an idea that has been fully accepted.)

From first point to last, the salesman backtracked or moved forward according to the way his qualifying queries were answered. He never repeated a benefit unless the answer showed that the prospect was unclear about the point or was skeptical. At such times he went over the point in different words and then used a different qualifying question or comment. And with his final query "Don't you think that a reliable second source of supply is sound insurance?" he clinched the sale. The close was almost a foregone conclusion once the first six benefits had been accepted by the prospect.

WHEN YOU CAN'T GAIN ACCEPTANCE

The more you apply the wrap-up principle in the field, the more you will appreciate its effectiveness in helping to clinch a sale. Sometimes, however, you will not be able to gain a prospect's acceptance on a major point even though you query him a second or third time. What do you do then?

This is a matter of judgment. You might try again and be rewarded with a favorable response. Conversely, the prospect may feel that you are stubbornly wasting his time if you persist after he has already brushed you aside several times. This means you must rely on your "feel" of each situation.

One thing is sure: you can't circle around any one point indefinitely. Move on gracefully when you must, leaving open the possibility of returning to the point later if it becomes desirable.

You could say something like this: "I'm sure this will make more sense after we have explored some of the other benefits." Later, if you get agreement on some related point, you could say: "Now that you have seen how this works, you may care to reexamine . . ."

ONE-BENEFIT PRESENTATIONS

Up to this point we have considered wrap-up when there were a number of benefits to present.

What if you have only one benefit to offer?

The principle still holds. For even that one point is meaningful only when your prospect accepts it. So make sure that your prospect has complete understanding and acceptance of that benefit before you attempt to close your sale.

Should his response to your qualifying query be weak, repeat the one benefit in different words. Then qualify him again.

A representative of a large drug wholesaler works with many small drug stores where space is at a premium. This representative writes: "There is only one major benefit I can offer that some of my competitors can't match: delivery as needed. But a frequent reaction is 'I am well satisfied with my present suppliers,' meaning in many instances that prices are somewhat more favorable.

"I used to give up on these prospects. Then I came to recognize that some of them did not fully understand the importance of that benefit. So I have been strengthening my story. Now when a prospect turns me down, I present the benefit again in different words. I cite what many of my very satisfied customers say, with their permission. I point out the reputation we have earned for keeping our delivery promises and coming through in emergencies. In a number of cases these prospects come to realize the importance of having a supplier they can rely on.

"When they reach this point, I qualify them on the total benefits by asking: 'Since you appreciate that we specialize in getting merchandise to you when you need it, won't you be able to do a better job for your customers without adding to your limited space or to your inventory, thus gaining extra goodwill, more trade, and most important additional profits?'

"Once they agree to this query, we become their chief supplier."

WRAP-UP HAS WIDE APPLICABILITY

Wrap-up goes far beyond selling. It may be used to advantage in daily communication, in civic meetings, at your club, and around the family table.

"In interviewing prospects for sales work in our Housewares Manufacturing Division," writes a sales manager, "I try to emphasize the forward-looking policies of our company and ask wrap-up questions at each stage in the interview to be sure that each point is getting full consideration. For example:

"1. Selling point: a company with young management and a high degree of decentralized authority. Wrap-up questions: 'What has been your experience in past jobs with regard to having authority delegated to you?' 'Do you like our way of operating?'

"2. Selling point: key employees compensated with above-average salaries plus incentive bonus based on performance. Wrap-up questions: 'What is your feeling about incentive compensation? Do you feel that it gives men with the greatest initiative and capabilities an opportunity to move ahead more rapidly?'

"3. Selling point: reviews of job performance, including a required annual review between department manager and each employee. Wrap-up questions: 'Our department managers try to have frank talks with each salesman as to ways in which the company can help him to improve his effectiveness. Has your previous experience included this kind of constructive evaluation?' 'Would you like such sessions?' "

THE MOST IMPORTANT BENEFIT OF WRAP-UP

I've worked in the field with over a thousand salesmen on observation trips in order to get a better understanding of the selling problems they face. Occasionally I've found men who applied the wrap-up principle consistently. Some had been trained to do it. A few did it naturally. *But almost always no matter how they came to do it, they were among the top producers in their respective organizations.*

BUILDING THE HABIT

The power of the wrap-up way of selling is indeed tremendous—much greater than is generally recognized. Yet any salesman can learn to apply the wrap-up method consciously. And when he does it consciously, he'll do it better and more consistently.

As with the other fundamental principles of communication and selling, the best way to learn the wrap-up approach is to concentrate on it for a long enough time to establish the habit. A month will usually do it, provided you apply wrap-up not only in selling goods and services but in all situations where you wish to get acceptance on points you have in mind.

Concentrate on the wrap-up principle every day for a full month. Before giving your presentation, list all the benefits you will be offering and work out in advance some of the qualifying questions you will plan to ask, thus assuring yourself that you are gaining more understanding and acceptance.

8

Objections:
The Key to Meeting Resistance

New salesmen often fear the objections that prospects may throw at them. The seasoned salesman welcomes them. He knows that once he gets them into the open, he can come to grips with them constructively.

As one representative says: "Objections give you a key to the customer's thoughts. Often they pinpoint the areas which interest him most—or least."

You can then build up the point or drop it, as the case may be.

Looking upon an objection as an opportunity helps you respond to it in a positive manner. You consider it seriously, answer it thoughtfully.

This attitude is often communicated to your prospect. Because you take his feelings so seriously, he will give more consideration to your replies.

Dig Out the Hidden Objections

While most objections will be openly stated, some may remain hidden and unvoiced. This poses a problem: How can you deal with an unknown objection?

To make matters worse, the prospect often conceals the hidden objection beneath a plausible-sounding excuse. As J. P. Morgan once said: "A man generally has two reasons for doing things—one that sounds good, and the real one."

How can you tell the difference?

It's a matter of judgment and intuition based on experience. You get to sense when a prospect is holding something back or when a stated objection is just a cover-up for an unspoken one.

Since you can't answer objections thoroughly unless you know what they are, you have to cut through the surface pretense and probe to the real source of the difficulty.

ASK A LEADING QUESTION—THEN WAIT

When you sense a hidden objection, you might smoke it out with the usual line of questioning. Should that fail, you can adopt a more subtle and often more potent method.

John Crandall ran into this problem when he was selling refrigeration equipment to a large Chicago meat dealer. His prospect listened intently to everything John said and asked a number of intelligent questions. Since John got acceptance on each point, he was positive the man was sold. So he was all the more surprised when the prospect said: "I'll have to think it over."

Sensing there was something on the man's mind which he didn't want to express, John said slowly: "I see. And is there anything else, Mr. Gordon?"

Mr. Gordon hesitated for several minutes. Then, smiling a bit sheepishly, he came to the point. He hadn't wanted to admit that he never made a major purchase without first consulting his wife.

Now that John knew the score, he complimented the prospect for working in harmony with his wife. Then he made an appointment to drop in on the Gordons at home that evening so that Mrs. Gordon could grasp more clearly the benefits to be derived from the installation.

Sometimes the surface objection may be valid enough. But if you are too ready to accept it or to go along with the "I'll have to think it over" put-off, you may often miss out on a sale that can be made.

LET IT BUILD UP

When using the leading-question technique, the waiting time may sometimes run into quite a few minutes—and a two- or three-minute pause can seem to stretch forever. But don't break the silence yourself, or you will spoil the effect.

Once you are sure there is something else, just nod your head in agreement with the stated reason, but in one way or another ask: "And is there anything else?" Then let that expectant and highly pregnant pause work on your prospect. Often enough this combination smokes out the unvoiced objection.

If it doesn't work, you can fall back on a direct attack. As one representative writes: "Sometimes I find it necessary to say bluntly: 'Mr. Jones, I sense that you have some objections to the proposal I have made. What are they?' This often gets all the cards on the table face up—and gives me a chance."

ROLL WITH THE PUNCH

Once you have uncovered the real objection—or the prospect has raised it himself—you must still deal with it constructively. The literature on selling abounds with suggestions on this score. A single chapter in one book on selling is headed "81 Ways to Overcoming Objections." Actually, all these 81 ways add up to one basic strategy: "Roll with the punch."

"I plowed around him"

Abraham Lincoln, who had a flair for dealing with people, instinctively applied this strategic approach. One day, after a particularly cantankerous visitor had left, President Lincoln was asked: "How did you ever get that stubborn old cuss to agree with you?"

"When I used to hold the plow," Lincoln replied, "and came to a very tough stump in the field, I never tried to rip it out. I plowed around it. So with this man. I plowed around him."

There you have it. When you answer an objection, you are in effect clashing with the prospect's views. You might win the argument but lose the sale. By rolling with the punch you avoid such head-on clashes. Instead, you "plow around" the man by first giving consideration to his point of view.

This basic strategy can be applied in many ways. But thousands of representatives use it most effectively by concentrating on just a handful—the four techniques broad enough to meet practically every objection that may be raised:

Agree with the prospect.
Repeat the objection before you answer.
Treat the objection as a request for more information.
Use a third-party witness.

AGREE WITH THE PROSPECT

No prospect likes to feel that he is being pushed. Nor does he relish an argument when he raises an objection. In most cases you can put him in a more accommodating frame of mind by agreeing with him first. That way he often accepts any change of opinion as his own idea. Thus by rolling with the punch you help him reach his own conclusion that your products will be of value to him.

The opinionated doctor

"I have been taking care of my business affairs long enough to look after my own estate," a physician said smugly to a banker who had been discussing with him the merits of his bank's trust services.

"Of course," the banker agreed. "With your background that's bound to be so." With these words the officer rolled with the punch and deftly opened the way to further discussion.

"Dr. Graves," he went on, "a busy man can sometimes miss a trick or two. Do you think a point-by-point check of your estate might be a wise bit of insurance?"

"Point-by-point check? What's that?"

"One of our services. We analyze the present composition of your estate, examine your portfolio, and make detailed recommendations for improving the condition of your estate. I wonder what your opinion is, Doctor, about such an independent check?"

(Note how the officer wraps up the point by asking the doctor's opinion. When dealing with a prospect who has strongly held views, it is wise to avoid angling for a simple yes response.)

The good doctor decided that the check had merit. One conference led to another; finally he named the bank trustee of a $300,000 trust as well as executor of his estate.

"Dr. Graves was somewhat opinionated," the banker reminisced later. "Had I not agreed with him wholeheartedly, I am sure he would not have listened to another word."

The banker summed up the matter with these cogent comments: "When a prospect raises an objection, he may have a case or he may not. But one thing is sure: if I tell him he's all wet, I won't get his business. So I agree with him. Then I dissolve the objection in a strong solution of benefits. I don't care if the customer wins the argument— so long as I win the customer."

Which gets right to the heart of the matter. When you answer an objection you are in effect clashing with a prospect's views. One way or another you must roll with the punch: go along with his views, then ease him gently into an appreciation and acceptance of yours. And, as in the above case, gain his acceptance by underlining the benefits. Each of the four techniques discussed here is merely another way of doing this effectively.

"That's exactly why"

You can sometimes heighten the impact of your agreement by converting the objection into the very reason for buying; that is, you not only agree but actually *appropriate the prospect's objections as your own strongest selling point.*

Hugging his objection to your bosom, you gently draw the sting—by using it to clinch your sale.

In one such case a prospect told an industrial hardware representative that he was entirely satisfied with his present suppliers, who were giving him just the kind of service he wanted.

"Of course you are satisfied with them. You should be; they are good outfits. But, Mr. Everett, that is exactly why I think you will want to hear our story.

"You see, I knew before I came here who your two present suppliers were. I would hardly waste your time and mine unless I knew we could offer you even more. But tell me first: Which of the two do you feel is better?"

"They're both good," said the prospect. "But one is superior in locating hard-to-find items and the other excels in arranging emergency deliveries."

"Exactly as I thought," the salesman replied. "You have given me the strongest reasons for considering my firm as your major supplier."

Then he proceeded to demonstrate just how the prospect would benefit from his firm's unusually competent service, using carefully chosen examples to clinch each point, especially the two the prospect had mentioned. While he didn't make a big sale, he did break the ice with a trial order.

When you agree with your prospect's point of view, you surely improve your chances of making a sale.

REPEAT THE OBJECTION BEFORE YOU ANSWER

When Richard Borden was marketing professor at New York University, he arranged to tape-record a number of real-life presentations at the point of sale. Sitting in buyers' offices as salesmen presented their stories, Borden and his students recorded several thousand presentations. Then they analyzed what happened.

Those salesmen who repeated the buyers' objections before they answered them had a higher ratio of orders to presentations than the others. *And those who restated the objections in even stronger terms registered the highest ratios of all.*

Why does this technique carry so much weight? By repeating an objection in sharper terms you have four things going for you:

1. You show that you understand the objection, that you see the issue as your prospect does.
2. You demonstrate that you are not lightly brushing off his point of view.
3. When you restate his objections so strongly, your prospect assumes you have a good answer in reserve. And once he expects an adequate reply, he creates a mental set which makes a good reply sound better.
4. When it is played back so strongly, an objection may often sound exaggerated even to the man who brought it up. Thus its importance is deflated even before you answer.

"Your blocks won't do"

To be told that your product won't serve the purpose is surely a difficult objection to handle. Yet representative Kenneth Armstrong meets it successfully by rolling with the punch. First he repeats the objection sharply; then he smothers it with benefits.

"In one case," he writes, "I was out to sell a prospect some oak parquet flooring. I pointed out the advantages of our 6″ × 6″ block, stressing its polyurethane finish.

" 'Your blocks won't do,' he said. 'I'm looking for a larger block, either 9 by 9 or 12 by 12, which can be more easily applied.'

" 'You mean that the larger blocks can handle more easily and cheaply than those I am offering?' "

(By repeating the objection so strongly, Kenneth primed the prospect for an equally strong reply.)

" 'True, the larger size will lay easier [agreeing with the prospect], but it does have a bad disadvantage. The block is one piece, and when the subflooring buckles or becomes uneven, the blocks also move. Our blocks are actually narrow oak strips joined together; this makes them more flexible. When the subfloor becomes uneven, our blocks can bend to adjust to the unevenness.'

"My comeback struck home. By repeating his objection and agreeing with him, I got him to listen to an advantage he hadn't thought of."

There you have it. None of these objection-handling techniques will guarantee the sale. But they should at least insure a fair hearing. And you always have a chance when a prospect listens to your story.

TREAT THE OBJECTION AS A REQUEST FOR MORE INFORMATION

Hundreds of thousands of times every day buyers are saying to salesmen: "We're not interested." "Our needs are well taken care of." "The product we have suits us very well." "This isn't the right time."

In a great number of these instances the buyer would

be eager to explore further or to purchase if he truly understood the benefits being offered to him. So it is that you can mentally translate many an objection into a *request for more information*. Just pretend a buyer has asked: "Does your product or service offer any advantage that warrants giving you all or part of my business?" This puts you in the proper frame of mind for a sound reply.

For example, a counterman was trying to sell a customer a scale remover. But the customer objected: "I've tried many scale removers with little or no success, and I'm not buying any more."

Instead of arguing the point, the counterman acted as though the customer had asked: "Why should I try again with your product?" He simply dropped a piece of scale in a glass of water to which he had added a measured proportion of his scale remover. When this simple demonstration provided the very pertinent information that the scale remover was truly effective, the prospect bought.

"It's too complicated"

"This duplicating machine seems too complicated." A salesman who handles this machine at times runs up against that objection.

"If I argue the point," he says, "I'll just antagonize the prospect. Instead, I look upon the objection as a question in disguise. I take it to mean: 'Can my office girl learn to operate it efficiently?'

"*So I answer the unstated question rather than the stated objection.* That is, I show him how simple it is to train his operator. Then I dwell on other benefits to be gained from that machine."

Here we see the two major reasons for treating an objection as a request for more information. (1) You avoid arguing with the prospect. (2) Treated as a request for information, the objection gives you an opening for ringing in more benefits.

"I can get it for less"

"In my experience," one veteran salesman comments, "I have found no better way of handling a price objection than by treating it as a request for more information. Since no one can always be low on price, I expect to run into situations where the prospect will say 'I can get it for less.'

"In such cases I know I have to show why he should buy from me despite the higher price. So I treat every price objection as though the buyer had really asked: 'What special features does your product have to justify its higher price?' Then I tell him in detail what those features are and what they mean to him. Of course, it doesn't always work; but it often gets me a sale I would otherwise miss, thus building my percentage of orders."

Even when you have the option of lowering your price to meet the competition, rolling with the punch can give you a good number of extra sales at premium prices.

"I've got all the stock I need"

Sometimes providing more information can be done very simply. For example, when a prospect said "I've got all the stock I need," one representative reacted as though he had really asked: "Why should I add to my inventory at this time?"

From that point of view the answer was simple. "The whole point of ordering now," the salesman replied, "is that our handy revolving display racks help you sell more. Each one takes up only 10 inches of space yet gives you six facings.

"Just last week I sold one of these deals to several stores on the other side of town. This morning I picked up re-orders from two of them [he named them]. If they can get that much turnover, surely you can do at least as well, or maybe better. That 10 inches of space will probably yield one of the highest profits in your store in relation to the front foot space it will occupy."

"After these 'I've got enough' objectors get this additional information," the salesman reports, "many of them decide they can use more stock after all."

Which sums up the whole point. When you treat an objection as a request for more information, you deflect it into a discussion of additional benefits. And that's always a superb way of rolling with the punch.

USE A THIRD-PARTY WITNESS

Often a prospect will raise an objection which if true would kill the sale. For example: "It won't sell in this area."

Tell him it certainly will and you're putting him in the wrong, which is always poor salesmanship. Besides, since you are an interested party, your opinion won't carry much weight. Yet you must get him to change his point of view. So to cushion the impact you bring in a third-party witness to make the point for you.

You may quote the witness directly or you may suggest that the prospect phone him. Better yet, if possible you may arrange for the prospect and witness to meet.

In one case, for example, Don Roebling was offering his house line of frozen foods to a large supermarket. "It won't sell here," the buyer objected. "I had a similar line before and it just didn't turn over."

Don had already pointed out the extra profits his superior line brought in. What's more, he had stressed that his suggested cabinet layout would induce most housewives to shop the entire length of the frozen foods cabinet and would yield extra sales on all the brands displayed. Thus when the buyer said "It won't sell," the whole thing became a matter of opinion.

At this point, if Don had repeated his story, insisting that the line would sell in sufficient quantity, the call would have degenerated into an argument between himself and the buyer. Instead, he brought third-party witnesses into the picture.

He could have done it indirectly by citing facts and figures from other markets known to the buyer. However, since his third-party witnesses were two noncompeting markets in the same city, Don asked the buyer if he would like to see how the cabinet layouts were helping those stores do a big volume on their frozen foods at a higher gross profit than the buyer's firm was enjoying.

Don knew that this higher gross came about chiefly through the effective merchandising of his whole line. He also knew that he could count on the cooperation of the personnel of these stores.

So Don let these third parties do his selling for him. And they did. The point? He personally did not oppose the prospect's views; the neutral parties did, which made it all the more telling—and selling.

A versatile technique. Third-party witnesses can be used in ways without end. They can provide evidence, as in this case, that goods will turn over. They can prove that the line provides extra sales instead of duplicating other lines. They can help you break through with a new brand or product by providing testimony as to its worth. They can testify to valuable applications that the prospect has never tried.

And why not? Everyone knows that a good testimonial from a trustworthy source is one of the best ways to impress an uncertain prospect.

On this score you can sometimes get written testimonials from good customers. These may carry great weight, for printed statements and figures have a high degree of believability. But whether you quote the witness, have the prospect phone him, bring the two together, or display a written statement, the principle is still the same. When your prospect raises an objection which you do not want to deny flatly, roll with the punch by calling upon a third party as a neutral witness.

One caution. Naturally, care must be taken in quoting customers or referring prospects to them: make sure the witness is willing and prepared to cooperate.

What About the Unanswerable Objection

Up to this point we have been concerned with objections to which there were some acceptable answers. But what if there isn't any answer, as can happen upon occasion?

You still roll with the punch. Admit the full truth of the objection quickly and casually. But *don't* linger over it; *don't* repeat it; *don't* underline it in any way. Just turn the prospect's mind immediately to thoughts of gain.

Suppose, for example, your competitor offers longer terms than you are authorized to grant. There is nothing you can do about it. Clearly, the more quickly you can deal with the subject, the better off you are.

So you concede the point promptly and briefly. Then you turn immediately to some important benefit that can offset the longer terms or capture the prospect's attention and dwell on that.

It won't always work—but it improves your chances.

The shipment was defective

George Lennox sells precision-made ground and polished cams, essential replacements for certain Swiss automatic processing machines. George tells about a situation that simply begged for this technique.

"I called on a customer who used to do a lot of business with our firm but who stopped buying from us very suddenly. When I introduced myself, he said: 'I wouldn't take your cams if you gave them to me.'

"That rocked me; so I asked him point-blank what the trouble was. It turned out that in his last shipment there had been an unusually large number of flawed cams—a result of faulty inspection. When he called the previous salesman's attention to it, he was completely ignored. That's when he stopped buying from us, even though the bill was eventually adjusted."

(Here was an objection that really carried a wallop. Still, the representative rolled with the punch.)

" 'I know just how you feel,' I told him. 'Had it happened to me, I'd have reacted the same way.' "

(He concedes the point quickly, making no attempt to minimize it.)

"Then casually I added: 'Do you know United Machine Works?', mentioning a plant in the next town.

" 'Sure I know it.'

" 'Just the other day Andy Jenkins, the plant manager [third-party witness], told me he never got such fast service on a complaint [bringing in a benefit]. Our Twin Forks distributor made the adjustment and delivery to replace a defective shipment the very same day.

" 'What I mean to point out, Mr. Bradford, is that our record of service and prompt adjustments of complaints is such that the experience you told me about is clearly unusual. Maybe that's why that salesman is no longer with us. Even more important, while some defects are bound to get through any inspection, Jenkins also said that our cams are more reliable than any in the business.' "

(George winds up his handling of the unanswerable objection with another important benefit. Result? Let George tell it.)

"After a year and a half of not buying from us, he gave me an order. I can assure you that if this customer ever has a complaint again, it will be taken care of immediately."

A MATTER OF TIMING

When should you answer an objection? It depends.

If you know from experience that a customer will almost always come up with a given objection or that he will have it on his mind even if unvoiced, "beating him to the punch" can be sound timing strategy. For example, if you know the matter of servicing is bound to come up, deal with it yourself early in the presentation. This minimizes it and gets it out of the way fast.

If an objection is a very real one, it is best to answer it the moment it is raised. Otherwise the prospect's mind will dwell on it, and he will not fully take in the rest of your presentation.

Sometimes, if you don't want to disturb the flow of your

presentation, you can say: "I will come to that." In that case be absolutely sure you make good on your promise—and don't let the answer be too far away.

Should the objection in your judgment be strictly an excuse, such as "I can get it cheaper," you can ignore it. But do pour on more information and ring in more meaningful benefits. However, when in doubt as to whether an objection is or isn't real, give it the full treatment.

BUILDING THE HABIT

You have undoubtedly used some of these objection-handling techniques before. But as with all the basic principles of selling, you will gain even more when you consciously build the habit of using one or more whenever the situation demands it.

1. Do you feel that rolling with the punch develops better relations with a customer than a direct attack on his views? If so, can you more often agree with him first, before you answer him directly?
2. Do you feel that the technique of repeating the objection strongly before answering puts the customer in a better frame of mind for listening to your reply? If so, could you start building the habit by using the technique at every opportunity?
3. Could you handle some objections more effectively by treating them as requests for more information? If so, could you compile a larger file of facts, figures, and cases in anticipation of such objections?
4. Could you develop more third-party witnesses—individuals on whom you can call for testimonials that

can be quoted in support of product or service claims, or to whom prospects can be directly referred?

Before each contact, determine from your knowledge of the prospect or customer whether you can expect him to raise some specific objection. If so, work out an answer to it before you see him. Even if it never comes up, knowing you're prepared will add to your confidence.

After each interview, review the objections the prospect raised. What technique or techniques did you use to handle them? Did you choose the best one or ones for each situation? Did you meet every objection to his and your satisfaction? If not, work out better answers for your next important contact. This before-and-after review will help you build the habit of handling objections constructively.

9

Closing:
The Key to More and Bigger Orders

You've been edging toward it from the moment you worked out your objectives. You prepared yourself with enough facts for a constructive call; you inquired into the prospect's needs; you sold the benefits; you punched your story across by wrapping up one point at a time, qualifying him as you went along; you turned objections to your own advantage. And every step has been directed toward one end: to ease your prospect closer and closer to the dotted line.

But all too many sales are lost only because the salesman stops selling precisely at that point. For no matter how convincing your presentation, your job is unfinished until you actively *ask for the order.*

"You never asked me"

Obvious? Perhaps. But the obvious has an unfortunate tendency of being overlooked. Consider the well-known exchange between Henry Ford and an insurance-selling friend.

"Jim, I just bought a new insurance policy," said Mr. Ford.

"Why didn't you get it from me?" asked the friend reproachfully.

Surprised, Mr. Ford replied: "You never asked me."

ASK FOR THE ORDER

Just as meeting objections can be capsuled into the four-word dictum "Roll with the punch," so the basic closing strategy can be summed up in four simple words: "Ask for the order."

Almost any representative will increase his volume if he concentrates on consistent use of the closing techniques with the broadest appeal. Of course, the more skillfully you do it, the more sales you'll ring up. This does not mean playing tricks on the prospect. A man who feels he's been trapped into buying will hardly remain a lasting customer.

By skillful asking I mean making the most of modern psychology and of the know-how which successful representatives in every field have accumulated over the years. For the way you ask can affect your ratio of sales to calls.

To help build a strong asking habit, you should focus on the five techniques that experience has shown will best meet practically every closing situation:

Assume the sale.
Use a trial close.
Close on a minor decision.
Weigh the pros and cons.
Make a direct request.

All these techniques are variations of the underlying strategy "Ask for the order."

ASSUME THE SALE

Nothing can put more dignified assurance into your close than an honest conviction that your prospect should and will do business with you. When you know you have something of value for him, that confident air should come easily enough.

Thus in effect you don't ask for the order. You just take it for granted. A wholesale drug salesman had talked with a prospect about putting in a line which he was sure would improve sales in the druggist's slow-moving cosmetic department. But the prospect was having a hard time making up his mind.

"After reviewing the situation," the salesman reports, "I was struck by the number of advantages the dealer would gain by taking my line. This hit me so forcibly that on my next call I simply assumed the sale without any preliminaries. 'I'm here to get your okay on this suggested initial order,' I said. The druggist looked it over and agreed, and the sale was concluded."

True, the case is somewhat unusual. But it nicely illustrates the important psychological factors that underlie this technique. For you can hardly take the sale so completely for granted unless you have absolute confidence in your product and your firm. This has a substantial effect on the prospect, who feels the product must be good to warrant such confidence. That's why he'll ride along on the same psychological wavelength.

One caution. A seasoned representative adds this warning: "Assuming the sale so naturally is a very effective technique, but when using it, you must be sure you know your customer's temperament. Some people resent any implication that you are telling them how they should run their business, no matter how reasonable your proposition may be."

But as the example illustrates, you can at times assume the sale even before you speak with the buyer and still not be presumptuous or in any way imply that you are trying to run his business.

When should you start to close the sale? You can assume the sale from the moment you are sure that you have something of value for your prospect and that you want his business. For example, a representative was trying to sell a customer a vacuum pump. The customer needed one, but his argument was that he could buy it much more cheaply from a competitor.

As the representative was discussing the comparative merits of the two pumps, he came to the point that just pulling vacuum was not enough; the pump must also dehydrate. The prospect accepted the fact that the competitive pump could not do this. Immediately the representative assumed the sale. "I'll arrange to have delivery on tomorrow's truck," he said.

Assuming the sale is one of the most powerful ways of asking for the order. Naturally, there must be adequate justification for the assumption, or it will backfire.

USE A TRIAL CLOSE

In one sense, a "trial close" is every closing attempt except the one that lands the order. But as used here it refers to every attempt you make to close the sale before you finish your presentation.

Slipped into a presentation as early and as often as the given situation warrants, a trial close serves several purposes. To begin with, it keeps you from talking yourself out of a sale. By irritating a man with a continuing sales talk after he's already decided to buy, you can push him into a disastrous change of mind.

To avoid this danger, you send out a feeler: a trial close. If the prospect is ready to buy, he'll say yes and the sale is made.

By the same token, a trial close serves to tell you where you stand should you be losing your prospect. His response will normally indicate if the point or points you have made have been fully accepted or if they need to be strengthened; it will tell you if more benefits need to be rung in; it may dig out any unstated objections which are still troubling your prospect.

If at first you don't succeed...

An industrial account used a special type of molding produced by a local man. While this product was of inferior quality, it was serviceable enough for the customer. What the local man produced one day was delivered the next, counted, and put into the inventory.

When an out-of-town representative approached this account, he had to overcome the important delivery advantage that the local competitor could offer. Naturally, he concentrated on quality.

"Wouldn't the men in your plant find this superior quality easier to work with?"

"Everybody likes a better quality," the buyer replied.

Responding to this acceptance, the salesman made a trial close. "When would you like the first shipment to come in?"

But the buyer retreated. "Oh, no; your price is too high. Sure, your quality is undoubtedly better, but the other serves our purpose well enough."

... *try again*

Technically, the trial close had failed. However, it furthered the salesman's cause in tackling the price problem. The salesman pointed out that his moldings came in waterproof packages which protected them against discoloration and dirt and that they were delivered as needed, thus easing the inventory load. He also stressed the saving from spoilage as well as the time saved in handling. Then he wrapped up the point with a qualifying query.

"Wouldn't these savings in labor and spoilage more than balance the cost differential while giving you the quality product you and the plant men prefer?"

"That could be," said the buyer.

Once more the salesman attempted to capitalize on the acceptance with a trial close, this time trying for a small order as an opening wedge with the account.

And once more the buyer held back. "It's hard to say just how much we would save. I think I'll stick with the present supplier; he's right at hand and that is good if any emergency should ever arise."

But this rebuff showed that the objection had shifted from price to availability. And for this the salesman was well prepared. His packaged moldings offered important ordering and inventorying advantages: all the prospect had to do was count packages once a month instead of in dribs and drabs every day with the loose loads that now came in. And he'd have to place only one order a month instead of several.

"Working with us in this manner would save you personally quite a bit of time, would it not?" the salesman asked, making his third trial.

And this time the close worked. After some thought, the buyer said: "I'll have to admit that it would save me quite a bit of time. So I think your plan is worth a good trial."

From this opening wedge, the salesman reports, the account has built up to the point that "we now get 80 percent of its business. Yet I doubt that I could have signed the account without using the trial close to show me which way the wind was blowing."

Each trial gave him a clue

Twice the trial close failed to get the order. *But both times it served an important purpose.* For the buyer's reaction to each trial helped put the salesman on the right track.

The first trial showed that quality alone could not be expected to swing the business. The second trial indicated that the benefits to the plant alone were not sufficient to justify changing the source of supply.

For the first time the salesman started thinking in terms of personal benefit to the buyer. This, as it turned out, was the key to the order.

"What if you had been turned down the third time?" the salesman was asked.

"I still had some cards to play," he replied. "I could have asked the buyer if he'd go in and look at the existing stock with me. I could then have pointed to specific types of spoilage that would be eliminated by our packaged product, thus dramatizing the savings. At the same time I could have asked some of the men how cleaner and superior stock would affect their work."

Err on the high side. That salesman's comments raise another issue. How many trial closes should you make? The answer will vary with the circumstances. However, it is surely better to err on the side of making too many than too few.

For one thing, as we have seen, each additional trial will serve to bring out specific objections which clue you in to the prospect's thinking. And more to the point: the more often you ask for the order, the more you will sell.

One salesman puts it this way: "Because it is all too easy to forget to ask for the order, I prefer to make trial closes early and often. You never know how close to a sale you are until you make the extra effort of trying for it."

CLOSE ON A MINOR DECISION

Closing on a minor decision is first cousin to assuming the sale. In neither case do you question your prospect's desire to do business with you. But in asking your prospect to first agree on a minor issue, you make it easier for him to make the main decision. For example:

"Do you want this leak detector delivered to your warehouse or directly to the job?" "Do you prefer a double-door box or will a single-door box do?" "Were you planning on the entire promotion or do you just want the display racks alone at this time?"

When you assume the sale, some of your confidence in your company's products or services rubs off on your prospect. By letting his buying decision rest on a minor point, you make it simpler for him to buy. Combining the two, as in the sample phrases above, is an exceedingly effective way to ask for the order.

Offer something against something. "The minor decision is fine," says one experienced salesman. "But it works even better if you offer something against something rather than something against nothing.

"In my own field, if I offer the automatic model on a minor decision like delivery, it will help nudge some people into a sale, but I'd still lose those who have no interest in the automated item. But if I close by asking 'Which model do you prefer—the automatic or the manual?', I'm now offering something against something—yet it's still a minor decision. Now, however, I can get action from prospects on both sides of the fence."

Since no is the easiest thing a buyer can say, why use any form of close that can be answered by a simple no? By offering something against something you assume the sale and make it psychologically more difficult for the buyer to refuse the offer.

Freight or express?

Regardless of what you sell, you can profit from this minor-decision technique. Capitol Records, for example, once recorded a series of children's stories based on the adventures of Bozo the Clown. The stories have been big sellers everywhere.

Artist Allen Livingston designed a rag doll clown modeled upon Bozo as described in the stories. Then he sold the manufacturing and distribution rights to a toy manufacturer.

Because of the tie-in, the manufacturer aimed first at the 15,000 Capitol Record dealers. He reasoned that if Bozo, with his floppy limbs and gay cotton clothes, sold well in record shops, jobbers and department store buyers would clamor to take it on.

The firm was sure that parents would go for the combination of Bozo records and Bozo dolls. But it didn't want dealers concentrating on whether or not rag dolls would sell in record shops. So all salesmen were instructed to close their presentations on this something-against-something minor decision: "Shall we ship them by express or by freight?"

Bozo proved a big hit. More than 40,000 dolls were sold in the first eight months. Undoubtedly, the biggest factor was the excellent product. But the manufacturer credits a share of the success to the minor-issue close that got Bozo to the dealers.

Use a combination close. In many cases you can assume the sale, make a trial close, and work in a something-against-something minor decision all in one package. Perry Miller, who sells a completely sealed hydraulic valve for airplane engines, tells a typical story in this regard. The unit cuts fuel consumption, lowers supercharger temperatures, increases flying range, and makes a greater payload possible.

After outlining two of these benefits to the chief engineer of an aircraft manufacturer, Perry felt ready for a trial close. So he assumed the sale on a minor decision: "When could you give these valves a tryout—next week or the week after?"

"I could do it next week," said the engineer.

He made it a series

Not that it will always be so easy. But you can vary the technique by paving the way to the sale with a series of minor decisions, each one taking you a step closer to the dotted line.

Here's how it happened in the case of a representative who was trying to sell a sizable shipment of rubber tubing to a new prospect. After probing the prospect's needs and describing his product, the salesman remarked: "We can probably squeeze this shipment into our delivery schedule for this area and have it here day after tomorrow. Would that be okay?"

(First minor decision.)

"Yes, the timing would be fine."

"Do you want this prepared for fork lift or for roll-off unloading?"

(Second minor decision in something-against-something form.)

"Fork lift."

"You mentioned that some of the tubing would be going right out. Do you want that material on top of the load?"

(Third minor decision.)

"That's right; it would help if I could get right at it."

"Well, Mr. Harris, here is a pencil copy of the order. Will you check the items which should be on top? Then I'll talk to the office and set up this shipment just the way you want it, and we'll also put a typed confirmation in the mail today."

"Fine," said the prospect.

(The salesman wound up the minor-decision series by assuming the sale.)

Many closings, as in the case above, are a combination of acceptances. Make each of these minor sales, and you are practically certain of getting the order.

WEIGH THE PROS AND CONS

Now we come to the most powerful closing technique. Used on hard-to-convince prospects, or thrown into the breach after previous attempts have failed, it often works wonders.

You've completed your presentation. All the ingredients for making the sale—or losing it—are out in the open. Yet your prospect won't commit himself: no matter how hard you try, he won't go beyond an indecisive "I'll think about it." To get him to move, you decide to add up all the reasons for and against buying, balancing the pros against the cons.

"Isn't it dangerous to bring up reasons against doing business when you're trying to close?" some salesmen have asked.

Perhaps. But "hiding" the cons will help you just about as much as hiding its head in the sand helps an embattled ostrich.

Your prospect has all the negative factors on his mind anyhow. And you can be sure he'll weigh the disadvantages against the advantages before he buys.

Then why not beat him to the punch?

When you candidly add up the pros and cons yourself, you keep the weighing process in your own hands. Surely you'll be as fair to your offering as your prospect—and perhaps more so.

The pros had it

Some years ago I accompanied an H. P. Hood & Sons ice cream salesman when he made a beautiful application of this technique.

On the way to the dealer the salesman told me that he had been trying for a year to get the prospect to switch from his present supplier to Hood. After introducing me to the proprietor, the salesman got down to the business at hand.

"Mr. Becker," he said, "we've been talking for a long time now about the advantages and disadvantages of changing to Hood's ice cream. What I'd like to do today is ·to review very briefly the pros and cons with but one thought in mind: Will *you* be better off with Hood's ice cream?"

"All right," said Mr. Becker, "but I'm not really ready to change."

Ignoring this, the salesman said: "You've told me that the main thing you've got against switching to Hood's is that you'll lose your present supplier and a very able representative whom you like very much. You're hesitant to do this since they have served you well for a number of years. Have I stated the case fairly, Mr. Becker?"

"Yes. They've continued to do a good job for me."

The salesman took out an $8\frac{1}{2}'' \times 11''$ pad. At the top left side he wrote "Cons." Then he drew a line down the middle, and on the top right he wrote "Pros."

Mr. Becker looked on quite fascinated.

"Since the supplier factor is so important to you," the salesman went on, "I'm putting a big minus alongside it, right under the cons." Then he continued: "Is there any other reason you can think of for not changing to Hood?"

"The customers like our present brand. They might not go for the change."

So another minus went on the con side for "Customers like present brand."

Once again, the salesman asked if there were any other cons.

"No," said Mr. Becker after some thought, "but those two are enough."

"Well, let's take the plus side now. You've had that promotional backdrop at your fountain about two months now. Is that right?"

"Just about two months."

"Do you think those promotions build more fountain and ice cream sales?"

"I'm sure of it."

"Well, you know that Hood changes these promotions every month. And regular promotions have a very favorable effect on your ice cream business. Is that a fair point, Mr. Becker?"

"Yes, I can go along with that."

"Then would you say we can put this down as a good plus?"

"That's fair."

"Now here's another thing, Mr. Becker. Do you remember when your ice cream case was out for 12 days? During that time you sold no packaged ice cream. Normally, 12 days would represent about 3 percent of your business. But since it was in the summer season, you probably lost twice as much. In line with Hood's policy of rendering top service, we would have put in a back-up cabinet during that period. Do you think that policy rates a big plus?"

"It's a plus, of course, but I don't think it's as big as you make it."

"All right," said the salesman. "I'll put down a small plus for this point."

Then he asked: "I wonder if you know how much of the milk sold in this area is supplied by Hood?"

Since Mr. Becker did not know, the representative supplied the figure, a little better than 40 percent. "In no other major city as far as I know," he continued, "does any dairy and ice cream manufacturer have the following and prestige that Hood has here. And that reputation, as you well know, is based on top quality and service. Everyone who lives in the area knows Hood as a quality house. We feel this could be a very important plus to you by bringing in new customers. What do you say?"

"Okay, you've got a strong point there. I'd like to think it over before I give you my final answer."

Now I knew from what the salesman had told me that Mr. Becker had put him off like this before. So I was intrigued by the way he met the situation this time.

"Mr. Becker," said the salesman, "here on this one sheet of paper we have the entire pros-and-cons story. On your own count, there are three pluses against two minuses. But let's look at the score a little more closely.

"In your mind the big minus is the act of changing: losing a representative and a house that have served you well. But this in itself does not put any money in your cash register.

"Now consider the plus side. Every one of those pluses will put more dollars in the till! As you indicated, more frequent change of store promotions builds more ice cream sales and store traffic. Keeping your case in service 365 days a year again puts actual cash in your pocket. And maybe the biggest money maker of all is Hood's reputation for quality—which means more new customers as well as satisfied old ones.

"And so, Mr. Becker, why put off a decision when this objective analysis adds up to one conclusion—that changing to Hood means more profit for you and your other stockholders? What do you say?"

After a very long pause, Mr. Becker conceded the case. "I must agree that I'll be money ahead. I've kept delaying this decision because Jack is a very good friend of mine and I hate to switch. But you've finally convinced me that I've got to do it."

Why it works. Weighing the pros and cons is one of the most powerful closing techniques, particularly for hard-to-convince customers.

Let's analyze just how it works.

1. When you candidly weigh each plus and minus, you impress your prospect with your fairness and with your confidence. This provides a strong psychological advantage. (Note how the Hood salesman kept asking: "Is there anything else on the minus side?")

2. By listing the cons first, you see exactly what you've got to work against. Naturally, you then make sure that the benefits you offer get fair consideration. If some benefits are minimized by the prospect, you have to build up the others until the scale tips in your favor.

3. Evaluating both sides of the issue reassures your prospect, making it easier for him to buy. In effect you tell him: "Mr. Prospect, I have placed all the cards on the table. You've seen the bad side; you've seen the good. Now you know that there are more and stronger reasons for buying than for not buying." That's difficult reasoning to shrug off.

He throws the biggest benefit into the balance

One salesman writes: "I find that I use the pros-and-cons closing technique more than any other. It is a very flexible tool, providing plenty of room to maneuver—to sum up, add points, bring out and overcome strong objections.

"When I stress the cons first, the prospect relaxes; this puts him in a good frame of mind to listen to the pros. Generally, I build up one or two good points to even the score. Then I throw my strongest benefit into the balance. Since the presentation has already shown me what the prospect finds most important, it is a fairly simple matter to choose the benefit I save for the clincher.

"I sell independents the idea of associating into a voluntary chain. And some of those merchants are tough babies to convince. I use every closing technique you can think of, but the pros-and-cons approach works out best for me.

"Usually I have to give three points on the pro side just to balance out their objections: syndicated advertising service, headquarters planning and display service, and coordinated bookkeeping procedures. When it begins to look like a 50-50 proposition, I throw in a big point: larger buying power with all the savings that entails. That heavy plus at the last minute will often do the trick."

No question about it: the pros-and-cons closing technique packs a powerful punch. It can be used to good advantage much more often, especially when you have a really tough sale to crack.

MAKE A DIRECT REQUEST

As we have seen, the basic strategy underlying all closing techniques is to ask for the order. In fact, most sales representatives use a direct request for the order as a major closing technique.

This can be as simple as "Shall I write up the order to include the promotional pieces?"

While such a direct request may not be as effective as some of the other techniques we've considered, it does work. For it is far better to ask for the order in some way than not to ask at all.

As the Scriptures say: "Ask and ye shall receive."

However, the representative who asks for the order directly has seldom fully assumed the sale. It was precisely this assumption that enabled the representatives cited in the above cases to use successfully their seemingly casual and indirect closing techniques.

This is not to say that the well-prepared representative should never ask for the order directly. Sometimes when every indirect attempt has failed, a frank "May we enter your order?" does the trick. It never hurts to keep it in reserve.

One may sum up the whole matter in a simple sentence: "No one ever lost a customer by asking for the order."

So one way or another ask for the order—and ask often.

When the Prospect Says No

In many fields the evidence shows that more sales are closed on a second try to a prospect than on the first. The question is: How can a salesman insure a favorable atmosphere for a repeat interview when he's just been turned down flat?

If you've made a creative approach, you've already

demonstrated your concern for the prospect's welfare. To get the welcome mat out for another interview, keep your eye—and his—on the same ball. "What I have learned today, Mr. Mardello, makes it possible for me to come back with a proposal more in line with your thinking."

PERSONALIZE IT

Most people will respond more readily to a made-to-measure solution. One salesman chalks up a good number of repeat interviews after a seemingly final no to an approach like this: "Mr. Andres, I can see that what I came prepared to talk about today is not what your particular situation requires. However, now that you have clarified your operation for me, *I'd like to work out a plan with your specific needs in mind: one that will do the best possible job for you.* I should be ready in about a week and will give you a ring at that time."

As this man sums it up: "I could come back without paving the way like this. But this method insures that the welcome mat will be out when I return with his individualized plan."

PREPARE FOR THE SECOND EFFORT

Making the presentation a second, third, fourth, or even tenth time presents a problem to some salesmen. They fear that the prospect will be bored when they present their story again and again.

Some years ago I was traveling on an exploratory trip with a salesman who sold several items, one of them a single-edged razor. We were about to call on the buyer of a small drug chain which had never stocked the razor, although it did carry the blades. I asked the salesman if he planned to present the razor story. He said: "No. I've presented the razor story to him many times. He knows every point that I can make just as well as I do. So I'm going to skip it this time and concentrate on those things on which I can get some business."

"Do you mind," I asked, "if after you are through I talk a bit about the razor? I won't be able to present it as well as you do, but I'd like to try, and you can give me a hand if I need it."

"Go ahead, Sid," the salesman said, "but I doubt anyone can make that sale."

I presented the story as best I could, and the buyer decided to go ahead with the deal. With the initial stocking order actually in our hands, I said to the buyer: "Jack has told me that he presented this razor to you a number of times. May I ask why you're stocking it when you didn't do so before?"

He replied: "Several points you just made appealed to me. For one, it is so much easier to clean than any other razor."

(At the time, brushless creams were widely used, and this was an important feature of the razor.)

"Then again, the fact that the razor has been adopted as standard on practically every domestic airline gives it a lot of prestige. While your advertising isn't heavy, I think it is good."

(I had shown the prospect some tear sheets.)

"Finally," the buyer said, "your store merchandising plan is excellent. I feel it will enable us to build up a good amount of additional blade business."

When we were out of the building, Jack turned to me

and said: "Well, I'll be damned! I've made every one of those points at least a dozen times."

Jack was one of the best salesmen I've ever traveled with. But that incident taught both of us a good lesson: never assume that the man before you really knows your story, even if he's heard it three dozen times.

ON REPEAT CALLS, BRING IN A NEW ANGLE

It is helpful, of course, if you can bring in a new slant on your next effort. A salesman representing an international publication called on a Cleveland firm to sell it advertising space. The marketing manager pointed out that the firm's domestic business was very good, and he quoted the figures. Then he added that its international business was even better. He gave much credit to the page of advertising which had been appearing each month in a competing publication. In short, he was very happy with the status quo and desired no change.

However, the representative did a fine job of preparing for his second effort. He pointed out that while the firm now enjoyed approximately 20 percent of the market, there was still plenty to shoot for. More to the point, the firm had registered consistent growth in each of the past three years, but it had made practically no increases during that time in its international business.

That did it. This time the salesman walked out with a definite promise of a 12-page contract for the same amount of advertising space as in the competing publication.

One last word. Many sales are concluded without a formal close precisely because thoughtful application of the other principles has primed the prospect for action. Thus a salesman who is having trouble in closing should reexamine his application of all the O PIB'ROC principles. For, broadly considered, each principle is a part of the close.

Follow Through for Each Customer

After you have gotten an order, you must follow through effectively. Build the habit of going one step further than your competitors. When you say "Thank you" for the order, let the customer know how anxious you are to serve him well. *Then prove it in the doing.*

After delivery, make a point of checking to see if he's satisfied; then check again later to make sure nothing cropped up to change his mind. Ask specific questions. Find out if he needs help in selling, promotion, applications, servicing, and so on. Above all, be available: keep in touch with his current situation, and arrange to be on tap when he has important questions in mind.

For the man who never stops working for one more piece of business, the close is neither an end nor a beginning. Tempered by persistent follow-through, it becomes part of a continuing process: a link in a chain that binds salesman and customer in a mutually profitable relationship. In this process the operative phrase is: "Follow through."

The president of McKinsey & Company spells it out unequivocally. "For too long," he writes, "we have equated salesmanship with the ability to sell the right man the right goods at the right time. Salesmanship does begin with that. But the effective salesman must have the judgment to follow up the sale in a way that insures satisfactory results and increasing business."

Follow-through on the sale breaks down into two tested procedures: (1) keep in touch, (2) radiate outward.

KEEP IN TOUCH

In this competitive era a salesman has no greater responsibility than to serve present customers in a manner which warrants continuing repeat business. For present customers are probably his best prospects for other items in his line.

Yet repeat orders are too often lost even though the buyer is fully satisfied with what he bought. Why?

Because the salesman loses interest in the goods or services he has sold. As one buyer complained to me just recently: "I seldom hear from a salesman after I buy— until he wants his next order.

"He does not ask if I'm getting proper use and service from his goods after delivery, and he never checks on whether I'm handling the items correctly; nor does he look in to see if I need help in moving them off my shelves. I don't like to buy from such a salesman unless I have no choice."

One man's system

In contrast to the above, one salesman has built up a solid backlog of repeat business by consistent and systematic use of follow-through. He makes detailed notations about the items each customer orders, the promised due dates, the projected end uses. Then he follows up on the outcome of the order.

Did it arrive on or before the specified date? What is the customer's opinion of the item? Did it work out satisfactorily for the desired application? Were any adjustments necessary? Is the service okay?

While this approach does take some extra time, much of it can be done on regular rounds and by telephone. More to the point, this continual follow-through pays off in a loyal personal following and increasingly high earnings.

There's no question about it. Developing regular, satisfied customers is highly profitable. And displaying an active interest in their welfare is an important way of doing it. You can write, you can phone, you can call when you're in the neighborhood. But one way or another follow through after the sale is made.

Follow-through is the best preparation

One representative writes: "I start making plans for my next call on a customer as soon as I finish writing the current order. Written notes and mental ones quickly converted to paper are the beginning of my preparation for my next sale at a later date."

Here I emphasize just one point: *following through on the current sale is the best preparation for the next one.* Consider this example cited by a highly successful lumber salesman:

"My preparation for a visit with the buyer at a large furniture manufacturer really begins by visiting with the plant's yard foreman to look at our last shipment, discuss it with him, and find out what did or did not appeal to him. After I get his views, I thank him for his comments and assure him that we'll do all we can to maintain the high quality or improve what he has indicated could be improved.

"Then I move to the buyer's office. Prepared now for the buyer's opinions, I immediately mention whatever I found that could be improved. I always commend the foreman for his suggestions.

"Following this pattern, I have now reached a point where the buyer expects me to see the foreman of the yard, discuss the past shipment with him, and determine between us what might be required for the next car. The buyer then confirms a release date for it. This saves him time and makes the foreman important: both of them appreciate it.

"I started selling at a very low profit margin, 5 percent. By watching each car and getting the reactions immediately, I have been able to increase the profit to 12 percent or more by shifting to more favorable items which were discussed in our follow-through sessions.

"Two years ago I did not sell this account. Today our shipments to it are up 50 percent over the first year and should keep on climbing. My firm is now able to make a good profit and keep everyone happy, thanks to preparation based on close follow-through."

He makes a periodic review

"The most effective demonstration of dependability and general interest is the periodic review," says salesman Peter Morrison. "Every salesman accepts the proposition that the customer is his best prospect for additional sales. But he fails to consider that by the same token the customer is his competitor's prospect. To protect your accounts, you've got to demonstrate your interest with consistent follow-through.

"For example, my main tool in protecting one major account is a regularly scheduled periodic review. This always has two objectives: (1) to see if we can service the account better, (2) to check out any new problems. On these review visits I often go out with the customer to talk over problems with his contractors.

"In one case I found that the customer was feeling the pressure of competition: he was losing jobs or getting them on low margins because of overbuying—for example, supplying precision-cut stock when random lengths would meet the requirements just as well. Once I knew the problem, I was able to work out a well-planned buying program that met every contractor's specifications, offered better profit margins, and put my customer in a class by himself as far as competition was concerned."

With that kind of planned follow-through, this salesman has kept account turnover down to an insignificant minimum in a highly competitive field.

He helps them keep in touch

Karl Bach of the Penn Mutual Life Insurance Company employs a unique follow-through device of his own design. Upon completing a sale, he invites his customer *to call him collect* whenever he has any problems or questions requiring immediate attention. In his book *How I Sell $12,000,000 of Life Insurance Year After Year,* Bach cites one of many cases where this policy paid off handsomely.

The story opens with a young man buying a modest policy from Karl just before being called up as a naval officer. After thanking him for his business, Karl invited the customer to phone collect from wherever he might be whenever he had any questions about that policy or insurance in general. From time to time this young man and his wife phoned Karl from various parts of the country to pose one or another query. Always Karl patiently passed along the desired information.

One day he received a collect call from New York. After a brief chat, the officer's wife came on. "Karl," she said, "Jim just got a big promotion. We want a $100,000 policy on him and a $10,000 policy each on me and the children."

That, you will agree, was a fine bonus for the willingness to listen—and pay for it!

RADIATE OUTWARD

There is one very obvious, very lucrative—but often overlooked—follow-through query you can make right after you close the sale. "Mr. Greene, you have seen how this plan will help you meet your specific needs. I wonder if you know anyone else with similar needs and problems who could be helped in the same way?"

This simple follow-up has meant millions of dollars to those who use it. It can mean many extra sales and dollars for you—if you apply it habitually.

"*I give them service plus*"

After you have made a sale, followed through on delivery, and serviced it well, you should begin to get a broader range of prospects. For a truly satisfied customer will often lead to the best kind of radiation: prospects he brings in on his own.

Jeff Ashford sells a maintenance plan to homeowners. This is a highly competitive business: if you don't keep an eye on the servicing problem, you can often kiss your customer good-by. "I get a lot of good leads from my customers," Jeff told me recently, "because I give them service plus."

"What do you mean 'service plus'?" I asked.

"Every firm in our field gives pretty good service. But I

add a plus: I call the customer the day after our men have serviced him just to ask if everything is all right."

"What makes this extra call so important?"

"Sometimes I catch things that aren't handled right and straighten them out. But there's more to it than that. These 'plus' calls show my customers that I'll go out of my way to help them.

"And it's a pretty good bet that they'll talk about the kind of attention they get from me when someone kicks about the poor service he's getting from another outfit. Or, if I have a prospect one of my customers knows, I can usually get him to tell the prospect about the kind of follow-through service he can expect from me."

BUILDING THE HABIT

The principle of closing means skillfully asking for the order with the closing technique that will appeal most to your prospect. The following questions should help you build a strong asking habit.

1. Can you, with profit, ask for the order more frequently?
2. Should you at times assume the sale at an earlier stage?
3. Could you advantageously use more trial closes?
4. Do you have in mind a sufficient number of minor-decision queries to meet your various needs?
5. When closing on a minor decision, could you more often offer something against something?
6. Do you think the pros-and-cons method could help you with more of your tough-to-close sales? Can you preplan one or more such closings?

7. Do you follow through in order to see that each customer is satisfied and to prepare the way for additional business?

8. Do you ask your customers to recommend other prospects?

FOLLOW THROUGH ON THE O PIB'ROC PRINCIPLES

One final follow-through habit will firm up each call you make and add immeasurably to your sales-to-calls ratio; that is, make a point of reviewing your application of the seven basic principles of communication and selling both before and after many of your calls. The envelope on the inside back cover of this book contains a useful device to help you do this—a convenient pocket O PIB'ROC card. In case the card is not at hand, a review of the seven basic principles follows:

Objectives: Set definite objectives for each account—for each contact.

Preparation: Prepare specifically for each customer.

Inquiry: Use inquiry to understand his point of view and his problems. Listen hard!

Benefits: Demonstrate with enthusiasm what you can do for *him*. Use figures, testimonials, demos, visuals, examples, comparisons, emotional appeals, logic. Consider the sequence of points.

Wrap-up: Get acceptance on each major point before proceeding.

Objections: Always *roll with the punch*. Agree with him, then answer. Repeat his objection, then answer. Treat each objection as a request for more information. Use a third-party witness.

Closing: Always *ask for the order*. Assume the sale. Make trial closes. Close on a minor decision—for example, a choice.

Weigh the pros and cons. Follow through for mutual satisfaction and more sales.

In applying each principle, consider your prospect—his point of view. Concentrate on one principle at a time until it becomes a habit! And, having once established the habits, check your use of these principles before and after your calls.

10

The Art of
Creative Selling

Once upon a time a salesman could rely on a quick tongue and a persuasive personality to produce sales volume. For better or worse, that day has long since passed.

Today extra sales and profits turn directly on the degree of constructive thought a salesman can bring to bear on any given situation. As the purchasing agent for a leading corporation told a *Fortune* interviewer: "We like to see the salesman who can show us how his products or thinking can help us out on specific problems."

That one statement underscores the two central aspects of the creative approach. (1) Place the prospect's problems in the center of the stage. (2) With his attention thus secured, shape your presentation to fit his needs as he sees them. 167

Supply and demand

Most salesmen agree that digging out the prospect's problems and doing something about them will open up doors to extra sales, earnings, and repeat business. The question is: How often do you do it?

Researchers have asked hundreds of buyers on whom salesmen call regularly: "What percentage of salesmen come in with a plan to be helpful—something that demonstrates a constructive interest in your needs?"

According to these experienced buyers, less than half come in with such intentions. As one man commented sourly: "Sales pitches are commonplace. But it's rare to find a salesman who shows genuine interest in your problems."

Opportunities galore

Now consider the reverse side of the coin. If most representatives do not rate as well as they might from the prospect's viewpoint, there are vast opportunities open to those who correct this deficiency. Such opportunities present themselves every day of the week.

In taking the creative route to more sales, you center your thoughts on two major areas: (1) get close to the prospect's problems, (2) develop creative approaches.

GET CLOSE TO THE PROSPECT'S PROBLEMS

To lay the groundwork for a creative approach, you've got to bring the prospect's problems into the open. And the more deeply you explore, the better your chances of making a telling presentation.

Truck salesman Oscar Chubb, for example, has become one of the top producers in his field mainly because he refuses to talk sales until he takes a long, hard look at the prospect's problems. "Just recently," Oscar writes, "I called on a buyer for a big trucking fleet in Milwaukee that was in the market for a couple of new vans.

" 'What would you like to show me?' the buyer asked.

" 'Wait,' I replied. 'I don't even want to talk trucks or trailers until I know much more about your real needs.' "

So Oscar arranged to ride in the cabs of the firm's trucks for a few days, studying workloads, stresses, gear requirements, fuel consumption, and so on. The potential value of the sale justified the time. When he called back to talk business, he had a truckload of facts and comparisons that the buyer was eager to see.

That started the interview off on a truly constructive note: the saving that would result from the modernization of the prospect's entire fleet. A routine presentation might have landed a two-van sale. The creative digging-out-the-problem approach opened the door to selling 16 trucks.

"Let's make sure we understand the problem"

Bob Olsen, who has built an impressive personal following via the creative selling route, sums it up as follows: "No problem, no sale."

"Before we talk about an order, let's make sure we understand the problem" is one of Bob's favorite opening comments. With that he launches into his inquiries, many of which he has prepared prior to his call. And since he is dealing with the prospect's own interests, he captures attention immediately.

Should the prospect start questioning him too early in

the game, this creative salesman may say: "Before I answer I want to know just what your needs are." Then he counters with his own queries.

Which makes it all the more impressive when he finally presents his case. By that time the prospect expects to hear some thoughtful suggestion slanted toward a solution of his specific problem. No wonder Bob is in the middle five-figure bracket!

They were bidding blind

Here is an excellent example in which the representative dug out a series of problems that the prospect hadn't even considered. What's more, the salesman helped to solve them.

"When a large contractor advertises for bids for construction in our area," this representative says, "he'll often get them from other sections of the country. I make a point of securing from the project engineer the list of out-of-town bidders; then I phone each of them in turn. I introduce myself, my company, and its products. At that point I inquire.

" 'Is there any way we can be of assistance?' I ask first.

" 'Thanks, but we're all set for everything we need,' they usually reply.

" 'Have you contacted all the subcontractors who will be sending bids to you?'

" 'No,' they'll say to that.

" 'Would it help if I prepared such a list for you?'

"Now I get my first yes.

" 'Would you like me to send you a copy of prevailing wage rates in this area?'

" 'That would be helpful.'

" 'Would you also be interested in the state and local taxes which apply to materials bids?'

"Another yes. By this time they're glad to keep talking. After all, I'm doing things for them that they should have thought of. So when I suggest the best hotel in the area where subcontractors will give them the maximum play, most of them take me up on my offer to make arrangements and have confirmations sent to them.

" 'When will you be arriving?' I now ask. And I offer to meet them so we can look over the construction site together.

"Later, I prepare the story on our materials and mail it to them. I enclose the current telephone directory, in the hope that it may be useful. If time permits, this information is hand-delivered.

"All this means that when the job is bid, I do not approach the winning contractor cold—*but rather as a partner who helped him get the job.*

"And there's only one reason I can do so. Because I got close to his problems by inquiring."

The italicized phrase goes right to the heart of the matter. By getting close to the prospect's problems, you may often help get the business for him, which normally adds up to an extra sale for you.

It's never too late

Many a salesman has experienced situations where personal or business problems lurk unsuspected beneath the surface. Bringing them into the open can be the one creative touch that wins or retains an account.

And it's never too late. The man who says no to an ordinary contact may well be open to a creative one.

Jack Armstrong, a lumber salesman, tells an instructive story in this regard. One day he was turned down by a buyer who told him: "We don't need any more supply sources." The prospect was a manufacturer who regularly bought 1″ × 4″ strips for crating office partitions and similar products. On his way out, Jack looked into the situation and found that the firm's high-paid workers cut the lumber into lengths of 30, 32, and 42 inches, which took up much valuable storage space.

"That gave me a cue," says Jack, "for I knew this procedure was costly. Talking the situation over with the mill that supplied us, I decided to make another call slanted not so much to making an immediate sale as to presenting a useful idea.

" 'Why not have the mill cut the strips into the desired lengths and palletize them?' I asked the buyer. 'You could unload by crane and return the pallets after you use up the stock. You'll save on labor and storage space too.' "

The buyer went for the plan in a big way. Because the firm had to invest in the pallets, its costs jumped initially. But after a while savings averaged between 40 and 50 percent over the old way.

What did Jack gain? A solid position which practically eliminated competition. But let him draw his own moral.

"I never make an offering now," he says, "without first probing for some details of the prospect's operation. By shaping every call around such highly specific information, I can tailor my presentation to the practical needs of each prospect or customer."

Creative selling builds lasting relationships

Obviously, getting close to the prospect's problems puts you on the inside track. But such exploration must still conform to the economics of the situation. In cases where present or future potential so warrants, your approach will require one or more exploratory calls. In other situations you may be limited to one call, in which case you must dig out the problem and suggest a solution in one fell swoop.

Whether you have one interview or several, you must still tailor your creative presentation to individual circumstances. And by focusing on your prospect's needs and problems before you talk product, you'll be taking a long step toward building lasting relationships.

The hit-and-run salesman will push whatever he feels will move fastest and earn the most now. The creative seller is also out for an immediate sale, but he keeps one eye on the future. He knows that there are all kinds of customers, just as there are all kinds of variations in his line of products or services. His job as he sees it is to make the proper match: the one that reconciles his own interests with those of his prospect.

Take the securities field. Merrill Lynch, Pierce, Fenner & Smith has marched to its preeminent position on the heels of one cardinal rule. As a senior vice president recently defined it: "Our sales rest not on whether we can make money in a given situation but on whether it is to our customer's advantage."

This creative philosophy is the secret of building lasting relationships. And to repeat: you can't make an offering to the customer's advantage unless you first take the trouble to find out where that advantage lies.

DEVELOP CREATIVE APPROACHES

Bringing a problem into the open can, of itself, often gain the desired competitive advantage. But the full impact of creative selling comes when you offer a solution as well.

In most instances a salesman can plan a creative approach in the period between his exploratory call and his selling interview. But sometimes he may be left with the task of producing a constructive idea on his feet. In either case, you can boost your percentages in the following ways:

> Be a problem solver.
> Extend your horizons.
> Develop generalized solutions.
> Engage in an exchange of creative experiences.

BE A PROBLEM SOLVER

In planning a creative approach, you must see yourself primarily as a problem solver and get your prospect to see you the same way. That's the most vital step of the creative approach.

Problem solving takes many forms. You may show a prospect an unsuspected application of your product or service; suggest a more suitable alternate; supply important information; help the prospect land an important sale. The possibilities are endless.

But the technique is always the same. Don't sell your product as a product; offer it as a step toward the solution of the customer's problems.

He stopped selling ice cream...

The Ice Cream Division of a large Eastern dairy marketed an exceptionally high-quality product. And Sam Halliday, like all the firm's salesmen, was skilled in bringing out its merits. Yet he was making little headway in the most rapidly growing ice cream market: the supermarkets.

Why? One day after he was turned down by the buyer for one large chain, Sam decided he was not paying enough attention to each prospect's problems. So he prepared a series of questions to ask himself before each call: "What product mix should this prospect carry?" "What proportions should go to novelties for children and to higher-priced items for the luxury trade?" "What promotional plans would most effectively move more ice cream out of the cabinets?" "Above all, what profit could the prospect expect for each foot devoted to ice cream cabinets?"

Only after Sam had put himself in a position to offer such a creative approach to each buyer's specific marketing problem did he emphasize the important plus of quality ice cream which would develop repeat business and cumulative profits.

. . . and sold solutions

Recognizing the merit of this approach, management, with Sam's help, worked out a new visual presentation which went right to the heart of the profit–promotion–product-mix syndrome. As all the firm's representatives learned to apply this problem-solving approach, their newly demonstrated interest in the buyers' needs began to hit pay dirt. Slowly but steadily the Ice Cream Division began overtaking its competitors, finally gaining firm hold of first place in the territory it served.

EXTEND YOUR HORIZONS

A number of cases cited above bear heavily on problems or solutions that have no necessary connection with the salesman's products or services. Why this stress on matters outside your immediate province? Perhaps a salesman who found the answer in practice can best explain.

"Given the sophistication of the average commercial buyer," this man reports, "desirable blocks of business may often swing on very narrow advantages. By falling back upon the careful planning of creative approaches, you can create such advantages for yourself.

"The more I range beyond the confines of my own line of products, I have found, the greater the leeway for creative selling. *And the greater my competitive edge.* When it comes to providing help on product-connected problems, my competitors can usually do as good a job as I can. Focusing on nonselling problems gives me an advantage because it adds a new dimension of service that my customers appreciate.

"Not that I know all the answers. *But by consulting with my home office and keeping my eyes and ears open wherever I go, I can usually be of help in finding an answer once I bring the problem into the open.*

"The prospect's production costs may be unduly high; he may be seriously limited in space; his inventory may be too big or small; his turnover may be too slow. Any one of scores of business or personal problems having no connection to my products may be bothering him."

This salesman offers a very good illustration of the advantages gained by focusing on a prospect problem that has no relation whatsoever to the salesman's line.

"When qualifying a large-scale dealer in the building materials field," he says, "I found he was interested in my offer but wasn't sure he could afford the investment at this time. I decided that I'd better investigate some more but arranged to see the prospect again in three weeks.

"I knew that my prospect's cash situation was tight

because of unusually high inventories. Now I wanted to know why he needed such large inventories.

"The answer was simple enough. The prospect's biggest customers were building contractors working on large residential or business complexes. They ordered materials in large quantities and wanted them on the construction sites when they needed them. Hence the inventories.

"The fact that I learned about this before I called again helped me go in with a simple but potent idea. I suggested that rather than concentrating on price the prospect consolidate his buying with suppliers who could give prompt and assured delivery. With this practice it was no longer necessary for the prospect to tie up so much of his operating capital in huge inventories.

"My own line? He bought without bothering to check out competitive offers—not because of superior quality or lower price *but because I was willing to look beyond the limits of my own interest to find ways to help him.*"

It is only fitting to end this section with an interesting case in which the very fact of extending creative horizons beyond the prospect's own stated boundaries proved to be the vital difference that clinched the sale.

The story begins when a meat packer called for bids on a relatively large job consisting of a meat preparation room, a meat storage room, and a freezer. The buyer stressed that price was a primary concern. Naturally enough, most bidders concentrated on shaving their bids.

But one firm had its own ideas: ignoring price, it concentrated on problem solving, for the prospect's specifications called for water-cooled condensing units and blower coils in the meat preparation room.

As every salesman knows, a prospect will often ask for something which does not best suit his needs. This immediately defines an area for a creative approach which can win out against more routine thinking.

"We knew this was not best suited for the job," writes the firm's salesman. "Instead, we quoted on specifications calling for air-cooled units and gravity coils. We explained that blower-type coils had proved unsatisfactory for other customers at the low temperatures required for this kind of installation. And employees complained about the cold air movement.

"In contrast to this, we included testimonials proving that gravity coils insured greater employee comfort and consistently better work output. Finally, we recommended that all units be installed outdoors, thereby allowing the firm to use the space allocated for a compressor room for other purposes.

"We sold this job to the customer at more than $3,000 above the lowest competitive price for the originally specified equipment.

"Why? Because we convinced management that the real point was not the cost of the installation but its efficient operation. By sticking to problem solving, we opened up a whole new ball game which put us in a completely different category from the competition."

DEVELOP GENERALIZED SOLUTIONS

When you can help your prospect or customer solve his problems without too much trouble on your own part, or when the potential is big enough, you'll rarely question the value of a creative approach. But a constructive salesman will also consider investing his time in a creative presentation—on low- or high-ticket sales—when he sees the possibility of adapting the approach to recurring situations. An example will make this clear.

He solved a recurring problem

Frequently, the effort put into one situation cuts down the time invested in similar ones. In this case the customer was unaware that he was losing business needlessly until the representative's on-the-spot study pinpointed what was wrong.

"A basic and recurring problem for me," writes loan officer Gilbert Snow, "is to convince my prospects that they need the investment capital we can supply. For example, the owner of a large retail shoe chain was sure he had no business requirements which called for additional investment. Yet my preliminary investigations convinced me otherwise.

"I knew that to tell him point-blank that he was wrong would be fatal. Instead, after some discussion I asked him to let me make a study of no-sale walkouts at his biggest store on Friday night and Saturday. This study disclosed that 27 percent of the walkouts occurred because customers could not be fitted properly and 24 percent because they couldn't find a particular style they wanted.

"When my prospect saw these figures and grasped their significance, he immediately became receptive to the idea of stocking a broader range of sizes in the basic styles which accounted for most of his sales, as well as a larger choice of styles.

"We financed these purchases. But more important *I was able to use this study to convince a number of other dealers* that they too could increase their volume appreciably by carrying an in-depth assortment of sizes and styles which we could finance on competitive terms."

As the italicized phrase indicates, the thoughtful salesman may well consider the investment of time—even on low-ticket sales—when he sees the possibility of adapting his findings to recurring situations.

ENGAGE IN AN EXCHANGE OF CREATIVE EXPERIENCES

The one best way to make creative selling a habit is to exchange creative experiences with fellow salesmen in your office, at sales meetings, or in your hotel of an evening. Should your contacts be minimal, you can still conduct your own private exchange by using the cases in this book as a foundation, for most of them have a constructive base.

As you read each one, you are in effect looking over the shoulder of an experienced salesman as he prepares for and carries out a creative approach. And almost always you will find at least one idea you can adopt or adapt.

His file paves the way

One salesman has gradually put together a thick stack of creative examples on loose-leaf sheets, which he indexes according to selling strategy or situation. "Some of these cases," he says, "have a negative slant. Many people respond well to this, acting to avoid the disasters visited upon the man who neglects his needs. Other stories have a positive bent. Thus for each interview I can review the kind of story I think will go best in the given situation.

"Some of these cases come from my own experience. Others come from swapping stories with other salesmen.

And a good number come from reading trade publications. Every time I come across a story I feel I can use to good effect, I add it to my file."

BUILDING THE HABIT

To sum up, a creative approach is one which centers around your prospect and his problems. It cannot just happen; it must be planned.

Building the habit starts with adopting a more creative approach to selling—making a greater effort to get closer to the prospect's problems and being more consistent in planning creative contacts. The habit will be strengthened further as you make a point of checking out the sources which help to make a creative approach materialize.

Talk as often as practical with others in the same or related industries, with suppliers, with those who attend association gatherings, and with your own company personnel. Read trade papers and attend sales executives club meetings. All these are sources for information and problem-solving ideas.

Most important: when planning your calls on major customers and prospects, give more than casual thought to how you are going to get closer to their problems and how you can solve them. Thus you will continually improve your ability to sell creatively—and profitably.

11

Selling Tools

Walk into the interview with nothing but a price list and an order book and you'll be working under a severe handicap, for some of your competitors will be making good use of various selling tools. Your products may be as good as theirs; your prices may match. But you'll still lose otherwise obtainable business to competing salesmen if they outdo you in this area.

Most salesmen do use selling tools to a greater or lesser degree. However, to get your share and more of the available market, consider how you can increasingly and more effectively apply the four most important types of selling tools:

Visual aids.
Demonstrations.
Promotions.
The telephone.

Visual Aids

Helping your prospect visualize what he is going to get brings him a lot closer to the dotted line. For this reason the most commonly used sales tool is the visual. This refers not only to the carefully organized sales presentation but to all visual selling aids in general. Here we shall consider the effective application of the following visual selling tools: samples, photos, and literature; comparison charts; and organized visual presentations.

SAMPLES, PHOTOS, AND LITERATURE

When you put a sample in the hands of your prospect or in front of him where he can see, touch, smell, or taste it, the probability of writing an order goes up appreciably. Nearly everyone recognizes this point, but time and again salesmen fail to use samples to good advantage.

Seeing is believing

A lumber salesman writes: "I have a customer who makes frames for upholstered chairs. He was using local oak, which he bought at an extremely competitive price which I couldn't meet. But I did have a high-quality ash—at a higher price than he was paying for the oak.

"I tried to convince him that ash, when surfaced, improved in looks. But he couldn't visualize it from my words.

"So for my next call I prepared some samples of surfaced ash. The customer immediately saw that this would dress up his frames tremendously. He tried a truckload and was able to sell several new customers at a higher price per frame. Needless to say, he is now a steady customer."

Another salesman selling a line of paper products presented a customer with the turnover figures of stores comparable to the prospect's. The latter showed some interest, but he did not buy until he saw how a display with colorful plates and napkins in a variety of patterns stood out against his other paper products.

Samples plus: the extra step

Of course, the prospect won't always be sold quite so easily, especially with more representatives preparing themselves with samples. However, a little ingenuity in the use of samples can still win you that all-important edge.

One man, for instance, got a lot of mileage out of a little extra thought. He prepared a display case holding small samples of spot welding of various metals. He asks his prospects to tear each one apart. They usually try out of curiosity—and fail. This gives him a clear opening for a constructive story about his welding equipment.

Double-duty samples. A salesman selling garden supplies very similar to those of his competitors prepared a setting of floor tiles covered with artificial grass. By showing prospects his assortment of supplies on this setting, the salesman was able to win over a considerable number of dealers who previously had used only competitive sources.

Preapproach samples. A little extra thought and ingenuity can pay off in any selling situation. For example, one man who depends on telephone selling worked out a way to use samples and photos in preapproach mailings.

"We do a lot of long-distance selling with our extensive line of wall and floor panels," observed this representative. "But getting the story through was not easy.

"The thought came to mind of sending out very thinly

sawed cross-cuts as samples to show off the fine grains of our most popular products. Photographs taken at very close range also proved to be of value in helping our customers appreciate the beauty as well as the practicality of these sound-absorbing materials. By the time I phone, this promotion already has many of the customers and prospects half sold."

Depending on how they are used, samples and photos can be visual aids, demonstration tools, or promotional devices. By thinking his problem through clearly, any representative can devise his own selling tools for various stages of the selling process.

Photographs show the product in use

Photographs of your products in action are samples once removed. Since many salesmen use them, the point again is to outdo your competition by using them ingeniously. As an industrial salesman comments: "I sell high-speed paint-spraying installations to manufacturers. Naturally, I can't lug a sample around in my case. So I have put together a photo portfolio of some of our installations which makes an excellent sales tool. The photos give the prospect an opportunity to see for himself what a beautiful job our equipment is doing for other firms. This has already brought in some good business and has stimulated considerable interest among buyers who previously had given little thought to such installations."

"They read my literature"

"I call on shop men with a wide variety of supplies," writes another salesman. "In a high percentage of my calls

I'll talk to my customer or prospect about a product on which I have some literature or reprints or both. With a red crayon I check those points which are especially applicable to the specific prospect. Many read this literature and pay particular attention to the points I have emphasized. I know because they often refer to these points on subsequent calls even before I get around to discussing the particular product. Since I adopted this method extensively, I have developed a sizable amount of additional volume. My customers respond to this extra service with orders."

By concentrating on it for an hour, couldn't most salesmen make much better use of the literature which is available to them?

COMPARISON CHARTS

Whatever you buy, anywhere or anytime, you never stop comparing. A store buyer or purchasing agent compares the quality of different sources, the suitability of different brands for specific end uses, price, and the reliability of delivery and service promises as against the actual record, and much more.

Surely, if comparisons are important to the buyer, helping him make them can be equally valuable to the seller. That's why comparison charts make excellent visual selling aids. They offer constructive service to the customer as well as to the salesman.

Comparisons shut out the competition

Richard Todt, a manufacturer's agent, attributes the success of his salesmen to "the care we take in presenting the strengths and weaknesses of our own lines and those of our competition. Among the firms we represent is a manufacturer of liquid detergents and spraying equipment that we have served for years. The entire line sells at higher prices than the competition. Unless the bid can be justified, there's no sale.

"To demonstrate the economics of superior quality, we prepared an item-for-item comparison chart which gives a clear picture of the longer life, more satisfactory service, and lower maintenance requirements of our line as against those of the three other major manufacturers. These tables also give comparative prices of all detergents and sprayers —our own and our competitors'.

"Because of the unusually complete story this chart presents, I have closed a good number of sales *without the competition even having a chance to bid.*"

He used a homemade chart

Normally, management will provide the comparison charts. But as this next case indicates, a salesman who wants to sell more can prepare his own. This man, who sells automotive supplies, uses a simple chart of his own devising to good effect.

He takes a sheet of paper and divides it into four columns labeled "Our Product," "Competitive Product A," "Competitive Product B," and "What the Difference Means." Then for each product he lists the specifications, features, service, price, credit terms, and the like for his own company and for two main competing firms. Since many prospects do not keep track of all these competitive differences, they often appreciate the information the chart provides.

Sometimes, when the differences are glaring, the chart

is not necessary. But often it has helped him land an order by highlighting just one difference when everything else is practically the same.

In one such case the chart showed that the salesman's firm maintained warehousing services closer to the prospect's territory. In another instance the clinching point was immediately pinpointed: the salesman's terms were slightly more liberal.

As this man remarks: "Were it not for the time and study that went into this chart, I myself would not have been so completely aware of the competitive differences that I can stress to different prospects. But one thing: everything on your chart had better be true or you'll be a dead duck pretty fast."

The lesson is clear. If the spoken word won't do it alone, then throw a comparison chart—or other visual selling tool —into the breach.

One caution. You can overdo comparison. Talk about competitive products and you are advertising them. No matter how objective and thorough your comparison may be, there is a danger that your prospect may regard your reference as "knocking the competitor." This he may resent, especially if his past judgment has led him to purchase the competitor's product.

It was probably for these reasons that the elder Thomas Watson, who once was called the No. 1 salesman in the United States, taught his IBM salesmen never to refer to competition. Comparison was to be left to the prospect.

Still, few prospects buy without comparison. Thus you'll be well ahead of the game if, one way or another, you offer your prospects comparison charts that at the same time justify your product or service. Such charts offer you five important competitive advantages:

They make your story easier to understand.
Customers accept and appreciate them.
They provide strong supporting proof for benefit claims.
They offer the customer a reasoned choice.
They suggest *action:* buy this, not that.

ORGANIZED VISUAL PRESENTATIONS

A well-planned visual presentation—a combination of salesman and organized visual materials—can tell a story so vividly and in so little time that most buyers prefer to be sold that way. As a study in *Purchasing* magazine confirms, more than 85 percent of all buyers find visual presentations more helpful and interesting than conventional interviews— and they prefer to see the salesman who uses them. More to the point, *they buy more from him.*

Consider but one case of many which bears this out in practice. Johnson & Johnson designed a visual presentation for calls on retail druggists who did not stock the company's extensive line of surgical dressings. As reported to the Sales Executives Club of New York, nine Johnson & Johnson salesmen used these visual presentations on 22 prospects who had been saying no to them for one to ten years. This time, all 22 druggists said yes.

A paradox. Most salesmen who have used visual presentations agree that they help to boost sales and earnings. Yet many of these same men who have experienced the selling power packed into a well-designed visual shy away from them.

Why this paradoxical reaction? Mostly because some salesmen consider the organized visual presentation a "canned talk" that reduces the seller to an automaton. This can happen when the visual is designed by a copywriter and artist who have had little or no face-to-face selling experience. It can also happen if the salesman is not trained to use the tool effectively—that is, if he is uncomfortable with it and does not use it in a manner that enhances his personality.

When these two hazards are eliminated, a good visual presentation can be a factor in helping a salesman to make substantial increases in his sales.

To illustrate: George Field, president of Renyx, Field & Company, wrote: "Sales of our Corporate Leaders Mutual Fund are up approximately 50 percent over the same period last year. The visual presentation is, I feel, entirely responsible, for two principal reasons. First, it has improved the sales of some of our established men who were weak in their production. Second, it has made recruiting and training easier and faster, so that the production of new men over the last six months has been greater than over any previous year."

Harold Gleason, chairman and chief executive officer of Franklin National Bank, was formerly with Hamburg Savings Bank. Describing his work with a visual in the earlier job, he said: "Before the visual presentation and the sales training that went with it, we closed approximately four out of ten inquiries for savings bank life insurance. Now we close seven out of ten."

Training your distributors' salesmen: double-duty visuals. A visual can do double duty—helping your customer's sales personnel as well as boosting your own sales. A leading floor-covering manufacturer asked me to prepare a visual presentation which would be used not only by its own salesmen but also by distributors' salesmen.

Conducting a demonstration for the firm's Philadelphia distributor, I asked the 48 salesmen present: "How long

does it usually take to present this line of floor coverings?"
After some discussion, they agreed that on the average it
took a salesman about 35 minutes to do a good job.

"Will one of you come up front and act as a dealer?" I
then asked. An old-timer stepped forward.

"Thank you. I am going to ask you to brief me on your
relationship with the prospect you select and then take the
part of that dealer. Raise the kind of objections that he
might bring out. Don't make it impossible; but do ask good
questions. Okay?"

The salesman agreed.

With the visual in front of both of us, I presented the
story one point at a time, answering each question and
objection brought up. I also got his acceptance on each
major point as I went along. Only then did I flip the page
to the next spread.

When the presentation was over, the men agreed unan-
imously that I had presented the benefits of handling the
line more thoroughly and more convincingly than they were
accustomed to doing. They also said that there was no
semblance of a "canned talk," but rather that the visual had
helped my personality. Yet I was timed at 21 minutes flat.

I then asked the men to count off into pairs. All were
given 30 minutes to review the presentation. Then one
member of each pair made a presentation to the second.
Even at this time, about 25 percent of them said that they
felt they had made a better presentation of the line than
they had ever done before.

Next the second member of each pair made a presentation to the first. This time a much larger number of the
salesmen stated that the visual had improved their performance.

Even though they had done very well on a first try, they

all agreed that they should not take the presentation out into the field until they had demonstrated that they could do a top-notch job. Each practiced with fellow salesmen or at home until he felt he was well prepared. When ready, he made his presentation before the distributor's assistant sales manager, whom I carefully coached. This assistant did an outstanding job. He did not authorize any salesman to use the visual in the field until it was evident that he could handle the tool effectively.

To help the firm carry out this program nationally, I asked three of its sales managers to be present at the two distributor demonstrations I conducted. These managers then rehearsed their presentations with me until I felt they were doing exceptionally well. In addition, I sat in while they coached several of their own salesmen. In this way, I was assured that they then had the ability to train distributors' salesmen throughout the country to make effective use of the visual.

The company had its best year. And its sales management recognized that the visual, and the intensive training that went with it, was a major factor.

HOW TO USE VISUALS EFFECTIVELY

Good visual presentations are designed to bring out one major point at a time. Because the appeal is to the eye as well as to the ear, the prospect can grasp the significance of each point faster and more fully. The visual helps to center attention on one point until the salesman can assure himself that the prospect fully understands it (the benefits principle) and recognizes that he will benefit from it (the wrap-up principle).

Too often companies send visual presentations to their

salesmen with no instructions except to bring in a lot of extra business. Not surprisingly, many of these presentations wind up on a closet shelf. Without instruction, a salesman may allow the visual to take the dominant role, thus usurping his function. He then does a poor job, dislikes the visual, and stops trying to use it.

Yet with proper instruction and limited practice the same sales portfolio can often be converted into an effective money maker. How? Consider the following four points.

Gain the prospect's interest first. When military leaders fail to do a good job of reconnoitering before they attack, the results may be disastrous. As a salesman, your reconnaissance effort is equally important. Without it, you do not know where or how to apply your sales points most effectively. Even when you combine your talk with visual approaches, you may fail to strike a responsive chord in a prospect's mind. If the first thing you do is bring out your visual, your prospect may feel that you are trying to force him to listen to a complete presentation. Nothing has happened to make him want to see or hear it. So he may resent such an approach.

Your first move should be to gain some understanding of your prospect's needs and problems. Knowing the nature of his business is a good start. Many times you can make helpful inquiries about a prospect before you call. And early in the interview you can ask questions which will disclose his needs and problems. In addition to bringing out valuable information, gaining the interest of your prospect in this way causes him to be more receptive to your story.

Such an approach may lead you to think that a prospect could increase sales or profits by having your product, or that he is having a problem which you are in a position to correct. Then you may say: "I'd like to show you how you can get rid of that specific problem. You'll see how, when you look at these slides [or this portfolio]."

If you sell typewriters, you might point out: "Many stenographic departments have adopted a plan which has improved both the quality and the quantity of their work. This portfolio demonstrates just how the plan works. May I show you?"

If you sell industrial products, you could say: "We have successfully cooperated with seven companies in your industry. For some, we have saved money; for others, we have delivered a better product; for still others, we have provided superior service. Usually we have given them all three advantages. Some of the things we have done for others in your industry are well illustrated in this portfolio. Shall we look at a few of them?"

Your prospect is then more ready to listen. He has a good reason to see and hear your presentation.

You have already planned where you would like to set it up or where you would like to sit or stand. You may say: "I can show you better if I move alongside your desk." By this time your prospect will usually be quite willing to cooperate. But you should know your visual presentation so well that you can use it upside down if it seems desirable to stay on the opposite side of your prospect's desk. If there are two prospects, it is usually easier to have them on the same side with you. You can then more readily give both the proper attention. If there are more than two persons, prop the presentation up on a desk where all can see it clearly.

If you have done a good job of reconnoitering, you will be in a favorable position all through the presentation to emphasize points of unusual interest to the prospect. As the interview develops, you'll probably uncover other points that appeal to his special interest.

Let the prospect participate. When you face a prospect, you have specific points you wish to put across. Present them one at a time, usually in the sequence in which the presentation has been developed. Concentrate on the major point presented on each spread. It will be stated in the headline or caption and perhaps be supplemented with subheadings. But *don't* read your presentation word for word.

For example, one spread in an industrial insurance company's presentation focuses on repair and replacement coverage. The left side of the spread features a partially blacked-out plant. The caption reads "Recovery with Usual Policy." The right side of the spread shows a full photo of the same factory with the caption "Recovery with Mutual Boiler Repair and Replacement Coverage." Pointing to the picture on the left, you could say: "This picture shows the recovery you get with most policies." Then, pointing to the right side, you could add with real conviction: "But this is the recovery you get with our company—with Mutual boiler repair and replacement coverage." Note that the wording is changed enough to eliminate the feeling that the salesman is just reading to the prospect. You will find that this technique will not present any difficulty.

In this case the salesman can now drive home his major point by citing local examples of losses and recoveries. Obviously, the more closely such examples fit the prospect's circumstances, the greater the likelihood of a sale. At various times a salesman can test the prospect's understanding. He could, for instance, ask the prospect if he knows about a specific local loss and how much that company saved because it had a Mutual boiler policy (applying the principle of inquiry to help the prospect sell himself).

The more your prospect participates in the presentation, the more likely he is to buy if your proposal fits his needs. The last thing he wants is to be on the listening end of a long monologue. You can assure yourself of greater participation by preparing queries in advance, keying them to each major point featured in your presentation (the principle of preparation).

Keep your presentation flexible. In this step-by-step procedure the well-designed visual gives you a planned sequence of selling points that are effectively arranged, cogently phrased, and dramatically illustrated. Nevertheless, you will rarely face two interviewing situations that are exactly alike. Each prospect's needs and problems differ in some respect from the next man's. So you should crystallize your presentation to help solve the problems of each specific customer or prospect.

To do this most effectively, you must know your visual presentation very well. Thus, when it is desirable, you will open up on point 3 instead of the more usual point 1 because your preparation and inquiry have revealed that point 3 will probably be of most immediate interest. In some situations you may not even refer to a point because you know it is not germane to the problems of the man before you. In short, you should plan your calling strategy in the most effective sequence and use your visual accordingly.

In instances where unusual flexibility is desirable, an $8\frac{1}{2}'' \times 11''$ loose-leaf binder may be helpful. You can tailor your story for different prospects by adding or subtracting pages or changing the sequence. You can also use transparent envelopes for photographs, sketches, and testimonials—all of which can be changed at will to fit the circumstances of a given interview.

Qualify the prospect on each major point. At meetings with groups of salesmen or sales managers I have frequently related various examples of visual presentations which have produced highly dramatic results. For instance, in a previously cited case nine Johnson & Johnson salesmen who had failed on many previous attempts to sell their major line to certain druggists made their presentations with the help of a newly designed visual. This time they brought home the business in every one of the first 22 presentations.

"What," I have asked, "is the reason for this seeming miracle?" The most common responses have been that the visual provides a better organized presentation, that it appeals to the eye and ear, that it helps to gain and hold attention, and that it gives the salesmen greater confidence in their ability to put the story across. All these points have a bearing on the results. But the most important factor is seldom mentioned.

All the Johnson & Johnson men were exceptionally fine salesmen. Long before the visual was developed they knew all the points in it. Each had used them effectively to win business from numerous prospects. Only occasionally did they fail, as with these 22 druggists. So what did they do differently this time?

They applied the wrap-up principle *intensively*. The cumulative impact of gaining full acceptance on one major point after another is truly enormous—much greater, I believe, than is usually recognized by most salesmen and sales managers.

Any salesman can, of course, use this wrap-up technique to great advantage in practically every selling situation, and without a visual. But with a visual, as this case dramatically illustrates, he can do it far more effectively.

APPLYING THE VISUAL

Timing. How much time should you spend on each point in your presentation?

This depends upon your prospect's reactions. With one prospect you may spend one minute on point 2 and six minutes on point 3. With the next prospect you may reverse the time element.

As long as the prospect is learning something of benefit to him, his interest may be expected to continue. But the moment he thoroughly takes in one point, you should move quickly and smoothly to the next. Otherwise he will become bored and feel your presentation is too long. He may even lose interest in your whole story.

When you work consistently with a visual presentation, you will make more comprehensive presentations and get acceptance on major points in far less time than you can in any other way.

Interruptions. Sales presentations are subject to several types of interruptions. The interview may be interrupted by another person or by a telephone call. This can be handled readily when you are using a visual presentation since the visual makes it easy to pick up exactly where you left off. If, however, the exposition is complex, you may find it desirable to review a point or two.

Or the prospect may interrupt the flow of your presentation by asking a question or raising an objection that is out of normal sequence. If the matter is so important to the prospect that he will not focus on the rest of your story, answer it at once, using other pages of your visual presentation as needed.

Sometimes the objection is not basic. For instance, while you are describing the benefits of a specific machine, the prospect might say: "It doesn't look as if it would operate as fast as my present machine."

You can often handle such an objection satisfactorily by saying: "Oh, that's one of our strong points. I'll come to that shortly." Then you can dispose of it in its normal sequence.

Getting ready for the close. The visual presentation helps you find the benefit or benefits which are of sufficient interest to your prospect to justify the sale. To uncover these points, you should usually make a comprehensive presentation. But once you determine them, it is time to close. If you can't sell him on the factors which are of greatest interest to him, you can't sell him at all. When you get away from these benefits, you are likely to lose him entirely.

As soon as you think your prospect may be ready, make a trial close. Often closings can and should be made without completing the presentation. When you get enthusiastic acceptance on a major benefit, make a trial close, such as: "Do you prefer the bright or dull finish?" That way, if the prospect is ready to buy, you do not endanger your sale by prolonging your presentation needlessly.

Using the visual on repeat calls. Tests prove that visuals gain a higher degree of retention than purely oral presentations. Since your last visit, however, the impact of your presentation has faded. Your story has been out of sight and is probably out of mind; your prospect has been exposed to other salesmen and products, some perhaps competitive with your own.

Your first job, then, is to lead him back onto your selling track, concentrating especially on those selling points that he may have accepted the first time. One salesman who has built an outstanding record of closing three out of ten repeat calls tells how he does it.

"Before I call, I endeavor to find new points which I believe could be of interest to the specific prospect. This does not usually happen. In any event, I select all the major points on which my prospect agreed in the initial interview.

For each of these points I strive to find some additional information—more often than not, examples of application or results or specific and favorable comments of users, preferably ones he knows or knows about.

When I tell him that I feel my proposal now conforms to the issues as he saw them when we first talked, I turn to my portfolio and take him through each of the major points I have selected, emphasizing the new angles and getting a reaffirmation of his agreement on each point.

"This serves three purposes. First, it puts him in a positive state of mind. Second, it gets him into the act. The more he gets involved, the more he feels that he and I are working together to help him with his problems.

"Finally, the new material or examples I add are closely related to his needs as he has indicated them. Thus my close follows logically from the *points he himself has ticked off.*"

DESIGNING YOUR OWN VISUALS

For the most part, management assumes the responsibility of providing comprehensive sales portfolios. But with some thought you can devise a visual of your own.

Actually, salesmen use the selling power of a visual far more often than they realize. One man, for instance, secured an important account with the help of a home-made visual presentation, though he didn't call it that. As far as he was concerned, he was just using a loose-leaf binder to hold all the evidence that proved what his firm could do and had done for others.

Two spreads were devoted to invoices, showing the wide variety of prestige accounts served and the breadth of maintenance services rendered. Other spreads had copies of correspondence, with key sections underlined to demonstrate the firm's willingness and ability to follow through in every way needed to guarantee customer satisfaction. Another spread emphasized the point with photos of maintenance men at work. These pictures and their descriptive captions, expressed in terms of benefits to the prospect, helped the salesman to expand upon each point in his sales message. Finally, a spread which featured copies of customer correspondence indicated that the firm could handle various maintenance problems promptly and satisfactorily.

In presenting his case, this salesman used the portfolio to introduce each point; he in turn expanded upon it or not as the prospect's reaction indicated. As a result, he increased his sales-to-calls ratio by more than 25 percent.

Make it fit the job. A good visual begins with a realistic concept of the job to be done. In designing (or applying) it, consider these five questions:

What are the key points of your line?
What are the key points for this prospect?
What are the conditions under which this presentation will be made?
Who is to be influenced?
What actions are desired?

DEMONSTRATIONS

As *Sales Management* points out, salesmen who have added demonstrations to their sales presentations have increased their sales over previous records from 30 to 300 percent. Demonstration is such a powerful tool that management often spends much time, effort, and money in demonstration spectaculars.

But here I want to discuss the plus an individual salesman can add by using a demonstration he himself prepares. This personalized extra has won a decisive advantage for many imaginative representatives. Often, for example, it can help you break through with a new line when a competitor has the inside track.

How one man broke the ice

For several months Pete Manning had been trying to sell prospects who had long been using a low-cost duct tape. His newly developed tape was easier to tear and had a high tensile strength as well as better adhesive properties.

Despite the obvious quality difference, Pete had been running up against price resistance.

Getting across the essential fact that the new tape was easier to work with clearly wasn't enough. There still remained the task of downgrading the competing tape. And this, of course, posed a delicate problem. Having watched it in action, Pete knew that the inferior tape often became unstuck. So he decided that a simple demonstration which allowed each prospect to draw his own conclusion might well do the trick. And more often than not, it did.

Here are some of the key points in Pete's presentation. Before making any reference to a demonstration, Pete poses the crucial question: "Mr. Bannon, do you ever find you must send a man back to a job because the tape becomes unstuck?"

Perhaps seven times out of ten the prospect admits that it does happen.

Thereupon Pete suggests that the prospect handle samples of both tapes himself. "Which do you find easier to work with?" he now asks.

Once the prospect agrees that the new tape is easier to

handle, Pete poses the final question: "Now that you have seen how much easier my tape is to tear and work with, do you think it would save your men an appreciable amount of working time and, most important, eliminate call-backs?"

Since many of his prospects agree, this method of presenting his own and his competitor's tapes has been helping Pete establish his brand solidly in this once difficult territory.

LET THE PROSPECT DO IT

With some thought, any salesman can prepare demonstrations which pull the prospect into the act, thus helping him sell himself. A retailer who sold a lot of ceiling tile was a big user of $1'' \times 3''$ stripping made from common board that had to be ripped in his shop. The wholesale representative won this outlet for his own clear redwood batten strip by means of a simple demonstration which allowed the dealer to sell himself.

The key to competitive price on this item was to use $3/8$-inch thickness, but the dealer objected that this was too thin. "Having anticipated this objection from previous presentations," the salesman writes, "I had prepared a demonstration. I brought in a sample of the strip from my car, together with a piece of common-board stripping and a stapling gun.

"When he handled my strip, he saw that it was stiffer than he thought it would be. Also he recognized that with the clearer redwood there was no danger of the staple striking a knot. When he experimented with the staple gun, he found that my soft batten strip took a staple well—much more easily than his common-board stripping.

"Once he had demonstrated the advantage of the redwood strip to his own satisfaction, he was ready to listen to other benefits: it would stay straight when applied to a ceiling joist; it would not eat up valuable shop time by having to be ripped; it had other uses—batten and board construction, pickets for a decorative fence, and the like.

"He took a trial order of 5,000 feet. He told me later that he appreciated the trouble I took to demonstrate the advantages of the softer strip. More to the point, he showed his appreciation by buying many regular stock items as well as the strip."

As in the first example, this representative's strategy was 100 percent sound psychologically. He let the prospect overcome his own objection by handling and working the product himself, thus proving that it would do what was claimed for it. Then he strengthened the effect with more benefits and finally closed the sale.

A demonstration establishes the vital difference

A prospective buyer claimed that one manufacturer offered a lower price on the same kind of air-conditioning coils as those offered by several competitors. If the specifications as printed in the literature were compared, the buyer was entirely correct. However, one salesman who was truly knowledgeable about his products believed he could demonstrate that his coils were superior.

To prove his point, he purchased a sample of the cheaper coil, took a sample of the one he intended to supply, and weighed each on a pair of scales in front of his customer. (Here the salesman could have strengthened the effect by having the prospect do the weighing himself.) In addition, he compared the number of tubes, the amount of finned surface, and the gauge of metal. This presentation enabled him to make the sale, even in the face of a 15 percent lower price by the competitor.

Because he went to the trouble of gathering the data for this situation, he and his fellow salesmen were able to use the same demonstration several times to win other orders. As in so many areas of selling, adaptation to recurring situations more than justifies the extra preparation.

A demonstration beats talking—and price

"I had been selling vacuum pumps and gauges for a number of years, selling my share," said one salesman. "Then I started demonstrating them by hooking up a small vacuum pump to a glass flange—such as that used in laboratories.

"This demonstration showed my customer exactly what happens to the water in a refrigeration system. It sure beats just talking about what happens. My sales of vacuum pumps and gauges have more than tripled.

"Usually a $125 gauge goes with each pump because we want the system to be dry—but we don't want the expensive pump used more than is necessary. Incidentally, since I began using this demonstration, I have never had to cut price."

He demonstrates by photo

A thread salesman believed that the display rack his company provided was far more effective in actual use than a competitive display. But he could not convince the buyer of a large chain of variety stores. On Saturday trips to neighboring towns he took Polaroid color pictures of all the displays he could find, both his and his competitor's.

From these pictures it was evident that in actual use the competitor's display was much less organized. The buyer called it "sloppy."

The latter took a copy of the photo demonstration into his buying committee with the strong recommendation that the firm change its major supplier for thread. He was convinced that the more effective display would produce far more thread sales.

In this case the salesman's demonstration went far beyond the landing of an important account. His sales manager had copies of the demonstration material sent to all the firm's salesmen, culminating in a marked pick-up in overall volume.

CONSIDER YOUR CUSTOMER'S SALESPEOPLE

Repeat sales often rest upon the enthusiastic efforts of your customer's sales force in selling your goods at the retail level. Here you can help boost your customer's sales by helping his salespeople demonstrate the quality of the product to themselves.

A few years ago, for example, a new type of foundation garment made in France was introduced in a Los Angeles department store. When sales did not come up to expectations, an investigator for the manufacturer decided this was due mainly to the sales personnel's indifference to the product.

To correct this, a meeting was held with the corset department staff. First a live model demonstrated the construction features which kept this garment from binding at the waist while reducing waist size considerably. Then the company representative invited every saleswoman present to go to the fitting rooms and be fitted to one of the garments in place of the foundation she had on.

It so happened that there were a number of mature women with all the figure faults found in a cross section of the store's customers. Since they were on their feet most of the time and did considerable bending and stretching, the women considered support important. Seeking support, they chose well-boned, heavy foundations.

So the new French model seemed too light and flimsy to give the desired support, and the women agreed to try on the new girdle with many misgivings.

Soon, however, they trooped back, amazed and gratified at the change in their figures. Tape measures showed their hips were reduced an inch or more, and their waistlines were smaller. Despite the girdle's light weight and boneless construction, the support was satisfactory. Dresses that had been too tight now felt comfortable.

This practical demonstration of the effectiveness of the new girdle laid the foundation for an enthusiasm that swept the entire sales force. Because of that enthusiastic support, the large stockpile of girdles that had built up was soon sold out. The buyer ordered a new shipment, and other stores clamored for stock.

The demonstration that sold the saleswomen generated the type of enthusiasm that counts. For while a good product creates interest, it is *enthusiastic selling of that product* that raises interest to buying pitch.

PROMOTIONS

Most promotional campaigns are created and developed by the home office. The salesman's job is to use them most effectively.

A wholesale drug salesman reports: "When our house was introducing a new hairdressing, the discussion at the sales meeting pointed out that the sale would follow if we could sell the promotion. On my first call that Monday I put it to the test.

" 'Manny,' I said to my customer, 'until recently this hairdressing was sold exclusively to the beauty shop trade. The majority of these professionals, who insist upon a better dressing, have been using it for years. This means that millions of women already know it by name—and more important they appreciate its quality. Many of them will be glad to buy it *once they know it's on sale.* Do you think that makes sense?' "

(The italicized phrase plants the idea that all the product needs is promotion. The question qualifies the prospect on that thought.)

"Manny said: 'It sounds good. But it will still take a lot of doing to catch up to the established brands.' "

(Once his customer accepted the idea of the promotion, the salesman concentrated completely on that point.)

" 'You're absolutely right,' I told him. 'That's the reason the manufacturer provides both outstanding display and excellent advertising. In its first year on the West Coast this item climbed to second position—with no other promotion or advertising except this display. And now the manufacturer has approved a substantial advertising campaign which will break in the next issues of these two women's magazines.' "

(Here he showed Manny the magazines, with copies of the first ads pasted in them.)

" 'In addition, Manny, here is the schedule of follow-through advertising in these publications. Wouldn't you like to give this proven new product a good play with display units on the counter and in your windows?' "

With this final closing query, the salesman tied selling

the promotion to selling the product. His effective use of the promotion paved the way to a good initial order and subsequent repeat sales.

This salesman sums up the point in his own words: "Breaking in with a new product has always been a sticky problem for me. Most prospects and customers don't want to rock the boat if they've got good lines and are doing all right with them.

"But now I find that when I sell the promotion as well as the product, I am much more likely to get a good initial order than when I concentrate on the new product alone."

In addition to promotions which the home office provides, the creative salesman can devise some of his own for specific customers and prospects.

Lighting the way to extra sales

A light bulb salesman writes: "We usually have great difficulty in getting volume out of variety-type stores. This stems from the disinterest of the clerks. In order to generate interest and create volume, I set up a deal with the managers to have each of the clerks wear a necklace around her neck. The primary part of the necklace is a tiny night lamp. When customers ask 'What is that for?', the girl is instructed to say: 'Oh, yes, that is to remind me to ask if you need light bulbs today.' Sales have skyrocketed!"

Initiating a million-dollar sale of chocolate

When a salesman from a chocolate manufacturing firm called upon the Toll House Restaurant in New England, he tasted some unusually delicious cookies with bits of chocolate in them.

Being promotionally minded, he reasoned that house-wives would enjoy making and serving delicious cookies like these. So he proposed that his company put out a package of chocolate bits with a picture of the Toll House Restaurant and its recipe for making the cookies.

The firm promoted this item and in the first year alone it sold over a million dollars' worth of chocolate bits. And the Toll House Restaurant thus became even more famous from coast to coast.

Setting up a redwood center

A wholesale representative provides this example: "There was a marginal customer of mine who I was sure could move a lot of our redwood. I really built up the idea because I was sold on it all the way. Our price was right and so was our quality.

"But while the man was pleasant about it, he turned me down. 'I've got too much capital tied up in redwood already,' he told me, 'and it isn't selling enough to make it worthwhile for me. In fact, I'm thinking of discontinuing the stock.'

"There was nothing I could say to that. But after I left I woke up to the fact that by pushing price and quality I wasn't selling the benefit he wanted. Because, as I saw it, I was talking buy while he was thinking sell. If I wanted to increase his volume and mine, I had to work up a redwood promotion and sell it to him.

"With that I asked myself the key question: 'Why didn't his redwood move?' When I looked into the situation carefully, the answer became clear: indifferent merchandising. In other territories our customers were doing well with good promotion.

"The next time I called I had a chart showing the sales volume that our other dealers were getting with our quality redwood. And I told him what we would do to help him get that kind of volume too.

"I explained that since there was no other dealer close by who was handling it, we would set him up as the 'redwood center' for the entire area. Then I outlined a whole program of merchandising and promotion: attractive displays, advertising, literature, envelope stuffers, and so on.

"This really caught his imagination. And by following through on everything we promised him, we built this up to a good account for redwood."

THE TELEPHONE

The telephone can help you increase your volume in many different ways. Just recently, for example, the Sales Executives Club of New York got some interesting replies when it asked 3,000 sales executives three simple questions.

1. "In which of these areas do you instruct your salesmen in the use of the telephone?"

To make appointments	80.8%
To follow up orders	68.1
To reach inconvenient accounts	57.2
To keep in contact with old customers	52.7
To reach inconvenient prospects	47.3
To solicit orders	35.1
Other	16.9

2. "Has this use of the telephone resulted in increasing sales efficiency?"

Yes: 84%   No: 4.9%   Don't know: 11.1%

3. "Has this use of the telephone resulted in greater sales volume?"

Yes: 70.4%   No: 14.8%   Don't know: 14.8%

Here is good evidence that you can probably increase your sales and earnings with the intelligent use of the telephone as a preapproach and as an aid in making sales and following through. An even more effective job can be done by improving your telephone techniques.

Consider this editorial comment from the magazine *Advertising Requirements:* "The telephone is such a common tool of business we just take for granted that everybody knows how to use it effectively. This is simply not true. There are techniques for the proper use of this instrument that can be developed and practiced."

These techniques fall under two broad headings: (1) telephone selling, (2) telephone personality and voice.

TELEPHONE SELLING

On the phone, as in face-to-face selling, the intelligent use of sales principles paves the way to more business. And here too the O PIB'ROC formula plays an important role. However, there is no need for another full run-through of these principles. Instead, I shall add only those thoughts and elaborations which pertain to the telephone particularly.

Objectives. "When selling by phone," writes a wholesale salesman, "you're wasting your time and money if you make a 'here I am again' call. And you also waste your customer's time, which is bad for future business.

"Having a specific objective before phoning will shorten

the call, keep the conversation on the right path, and help to close the sale. Personally, I not only have a specific aim in terms of what I want to sell; I also try to have some constructive idea for the customer."

Preparation. "What is the most important factor in telephone selling?" I have asked a number of salesmen who do nearly all their selling by phone.

"Adequate preparation," the majority have replied. Here are three typical comments.

Says one man: "Preparation before making my calls is perhaps the single biggest item in writing up more orders. When combined with service, quality, and competitive pricing, it keeps me on an equal footing with the in-person salesman."

A second man, who has a number of telephone representatives working under him, remarks: "Given several men with equal knowledge of the products and of the market, the fellow who is best prepared to suggest various product applications without stopping to look things up will far outsell the others."

The third man sums it up like this: "In telephone selling you've got to make your points quickly and without fumbling. If you keep the customer dangling because you're not prepared, you're dead."

"Organize your desk"

The salesman just cited goes on to say: "Sometimes you can do a good job off the cuff. But don't count on it; organize your desk and be sure.

"I make a practice of briefing every point I want to put across and have my notes on my desk before I pick up the phone. I keep records of previous correspondence and conversations close at hand; I have alternates lined up and priced in case I have to use them; and I try to anticipate customer objections. If the customer is important enough, I have all this material typed in outline form."

"I had one prospect," a telephone salesman told me, "who said flatly that a telephone salesman could not give him the kind of personal service he desired—the kind he could get from a local man. During this conversation I made note of his comment that he would gladly pay an extra dollar for quality since that was his strongest selling point to his customers. He also said that one of his best customers was in the market for several compressors which were to be exposed in use.

"After I had checked out the situation thoroughly, I called the prospect back with my complete notes in front of me. Referring to his customer who was in the market for compressors, I said: 'He's going to use them exposed? Is that right?'

" 'That's right.'

" 'In that case, you might suggest that he can insure a good start-up and lubrication on the starter with a top-quality crankcase heater that I located since I talked with you.'

" 'That's a very good point,' said the prospect.

" 'In addition, I have checked out the specifications on compressors in the price range you mentioned and I have one that I believe will do the best possible job for your customer under the conditions you described.'

"When I brought out the quality features which I was able to give him at a competitive price, I got a firm order. More to the point, he told me that I had convinced him that a telephone salesman could give him the kind of service he required. And I made that sale only because I prepared myself to be constructive."

Actually, the telephone salesman has an edge here. He can have far more information at his fingertips than the outside salesman can carry in his briefcase. Specifications, comparative prices, customer records, past conversations and correspondence with the prospect, end uses and applications, materials currently in stock, delivery times on other items—all this information and more can be within immediate reach. The main problem is to organize that material and your desk so effectively that you can promptly put your finger on what you want as needed, thus avoiding fatal silences while you look for the data.

Before making a call, it is good practice to have in your notes questions you plan to ask the prospect—questions designed to get a better understanding of his needs and his problems or questions designed to gain his interest.

Benefits. Selling the benefits poses a real problem in telephone selling. For if the benefits don't come through to the man on the other end of the wire, neither will the order. Yet you can't show the prospect a sample or physically demonstrate the superiority of your product.

Despite such handicaps, telephone salesmen do punch home the benefits every day of the week. And they do it most effectively when they develop benefit "briefs" to keep as handy guides to the sale.

Some years ago, for example, when throwaway ballpoint pens were introduced, the salesmen of one large distributor did much of their selling by phone. Dealers were showing resistance because they feared that the reduced demand for refills would cut down their sales and profits. The presentations were made around this well-thought-out benefit brief typed in outline form:

"1. Because it's a new product, the manufacturer has scheduled a national promotion and we are tying in with local advertising.

"2. This promotion on the 'throwaway' theme *is bound to bring in customers* asking for the no-refill pen.

"3. Because more customers will walk into your store, they will see your other items and displays, especially stationery. This means that you will get much more all-around business.

"4. Sure, you'll sell fewer refills—but you'll be selling throwaway pens instead, and making more profit."

Using this benefit brief as a guide and expanding upon each point as needed, the distributor's salesmen chalked up an impressive number of sales well before the promotion campaign put the product over on a national scale.

Briefs have assisted many telephone salesmen in bringing out the benefits logically, forcibly, and with a minimum of words. And you can gain a greater impact by building word pictures, using highly descriptive words and phrases.

Look, for example, at point 3 of the benefit brief just cited. The face-to-face salesman could have said: "With this promotion your store traffic will increase." And in face-to-face selling that could do the trick.

But on the telephone, where you appeal only to the sense of hearing, you need to do a better job and build a more definite picture in his mind. That's what the telephone brief did. "More customers will walk into your store" draws a more definite picture. The picture is further clarified by "they will see your other items and displays, especially stationery, which means you will get more all-around business."

In a word, give your telephone customer a clearer picture of benefits by avoiding generalities. Instead, provide precise details on time, place, materials, figures—and anything he can *visualize* in picture form.

Your presentation will then help him fully appreciate what your product and services will do for him.

Wrap-up. No matter how detailed and descriptive your benefit brief, on the phone you still can't be sure that it's getting across—that your customer understands and accepts each major point. Your best bet is to get a playback: to qualify him point by point as you go through your brief. And you'll take the guesswork out of it if you prepare your qualifying queries beforehand and get full acceptance on each major point before you proceed to the next.

He sells prepackaged paneling

One representative follows this wrap-up procedure when he sells prepackaged paneling by phone. "First," he says, "I list the seven benefits I want to put into the prospect's mind. These are:

1. Stock can be bought in 7-, 8-, and 10-foot packages.
2. It's easy to handle.
3. Stock stays clean.
4. There is less picking over in the yard.
5. It has eye appeal for your customers.
6. There is less likelihood of remnants being sent back.
7. It's easy to inventory.

"Then I prepare my qualifying queries for each point: 'Dealers have told me that this prepackaged paneling cuts their handling costs by more than half. Would it in your case?' 'How much do you think this clean quality stock would add to your sales?'

"And so on down the line. Only by making frequent

stops to see if my prospect is keeping up with me can I be sure he is getting a full appreciation of each benefit."

Such qualifying queries serve another good purpose on the phone. They help you make sure your customer *hears* what you say. He has to, in order to accept—or reject—it.

Finally, on the phone more than in face-to-face selling, people resent listening to a monologue, so keep your sentences short. Use adroit wrap-up questions. Plan to elicit more than just a yes-or-no response. Prepare queries that provoke two-way discussion. This mutual participation will add another plus to the many factors which can make or break a sale.

Objections. Before you pick up the phone, list or have clearly in mind those objections your prospect is apt to raise. Figure out how you will meet them in terms of his special needs and interests. You can then welcome his objections, because as you satisfy each one you will be getting closer to the sale.

Closing. The principle of closing requires that, if needed, you ask for the order—a step which is surprisingly often neglected by both face-to-face and telephone salesmen. On the phone adding the pros and cons (see Chapter 9) is an excellent way of getting the prospect to visualize what he will gain by buying.

TELEPHONE PERSONALITY AND VOICE

Besides adequate preparation and the adroit use of principles, telephone selling (and face-to-face selling) can be greatly enhanced by the acquisition of a pleasant and forceful speaking voice.

In New York City one organization devotes its primary attention to assisting those who sell in making better use of their voices. Among others, the firm has served a number of life insurance agencies which hire professional telephone sales personnel to call prospects and make appointments for face-to-face salesmen.

After being trained in the use of their voices, these salespeople increased their ratio of appointments to calls by 25 to 50 percent, and in some cases even more.

Everything else remained the same: the same briefs, the same salespeople, the same lists. The only thing that changed was the voice. And when you consider that these telephone salespeople were professionals, the results indicate the tremendous effect that proper use of the voice can have on sales.

Fortunately, almost everyone who desires can learn to make better use of his voice. You can do it within a few weeks by practicing these three simple exercises:

1. Sound every letter of every word you utter. On your first try you will find yourself enunciating more clearly. And with practice your enunciation will further improve. A good time to do this is when you are in your car alone. For then you take no time from other activities.

2. Put more color into your voice—more highs, more lows, and more pauses. Low tones are more pleasing and should be cultivated. Practice putting extra color into your voice while you are sounding every letter—that is, express more feeling for the thought you are conveying and especially add more dramatic pauses. Try it, and you'll see that it presents no problem.

3. Use more of your voice apparatus. Observe TV announcers and singers. Note how much their lips and jaws move. Too many of us swallow our words and they do not come out clearly.

When you use more of your voice apparatus, your voice

box, or larynx, actually enlarges and you get more reso-
nance.

As you are riding in your car alone, talk in a strong
whisper as if you wanted to be heard clearly by someone
as much as 25 or 50 feet away. Do this for a sentence or
two. You will then be using your voice apparatus much
more fully. Now change to your normal voice, continuing
to use your voice apparatus. Practice this step long enough
to develop the habit, and your speech will more and more
resemble that of a good TV announcer.

Salesmen and sales managers who have practiced these
three steps for as little as two or three weeks have reported
significant results. A mortgage officer in a bank, for instance, was told by one of his friends: "This is the third
time I have heard you talk on mortgage financing. This
last one was a much more informative talk." Yet the mortgage officer claims that it was the same speech. The only
change was in the voice.

One salesman practiced for several weeks without telling anybody about it. After a gathering at his home, his
wife said: "Frank, you have always done your share and
more in carrying on the conversation when our friends
come in, but recently you have become much more interesting." Frank asserts that the only difference was the way
in which he used his voice.

Projecting warmth. Face to face, you can appeal to all
five senses. Your customer can see and hear you. He can
touch the samples you are presenting. He can smell your
cigarette or taste the lunch you may be buying.

When selling by phone, you must depend on your voice
alone. Despite this limitation, many telephone salesmen
who seldom see their customers build relationships that are

almost as cordial as those developed by outside salesmen.

For one thing, they know how to *project warmth* through the voice. They know it is a fact that when they smile as they talk *the smile will come through at the other end of the wire*. But it has to be genuine. Many professional salesmen who spend most of their time on the phone place a mirror nearby so that they can see their smile in it. The mirror helps to keep them in a smiling mood.

There's one other factor vital to projecting warmth: visualize the person you are talking to.

What accounts for so much of cool telephone detachment? We forget there's a person, a human being, attached to the voice we're listening and talking to. Visualize your customer at the other end—his face, his hands, his gestures —and your natural warmth will surely assert itself.

BUILDING THE HABIT

Habit-building follow-through in the use of selling tools will be most productive when it becomes part of your written objectives—and when you live those objectives day by day, week by week, and month by month. As you prepare your calls on important prospects and customers, consider the following points:

1. Exactly how can you use existing visual aids to greater advantage? Can you make them more meaningful by adding local material? Can you develop one to fit your own special selling circumstances?
2. What about demonstrations? Will you use them more often? Will you develop your own?

3. Can you help your customers move their products faster with company promotions? With promotions you devise? Can you make more sales by selling more promotions?

4. Do you need to focus on more consistent use of the O PIB'ROC principles on the telephone? Do you plan to practice the voice-improvement exercises?

12

Recurring Situations

Salesmen usually spend most of their effort on recurring situations, situations which are sufficiently similar to warrant developing a strategy for dealing with them. In selling to industrial firms, for example, a salesman faces the same competition he has previously met. In selling to retail outlets, a representative may have to cope with the objection "We have all the brands we require to meet our needs." Or an oil company salesman may find his volume falling only because a number of his station operators fail to carry through sufficiently on promotions.

One salesman may regard these troublesome recurring situations as nuisances. Another may recognize them as opportunities. For the very fact that a situation does recur so often means that a strategy dealing with it successfully in one case can pay off in multiple sales if it is adapted and applied to other prospects and customers.

The recurring situation may be a prospect objection; it may be skepticism on the quality of a new product or brand; it may be doubt about the firm's dependability on service. Whatever the situation, you keep running into it time and again—and it cuts deeply into your sales-to-calls ratio. That's the signal to stop and do something about it—now.

Regardless of the difficulty you run up against regularly, you can best come to terms with it by applying the same step-by-step method that underlies the creative approach.

1. List your recurring roadblocks. Include all those which crop up often enough to warrant working out a strategy for dealing with them.
2. Arrange them in order of importance, with the one which most adversely affects your earnings rated first, and so on.
3. Concentrate on the first situation long enough to work out a strategy for handling it which registers significant improvement as you begin to apply it.
4. Check your improved strategy with your sales manager and your fellow salesmen.
5. When you have an approach that works and have built the habit of using it effectively, move on to the second roadblock and focus on it. Continue in this fashion until you have covered every recurring situation.

Both for convenience and because there is an important difference between the two, we shall consider recurring situations under two broad headings: (1) recurring selling situations which can be dealt with directly in your presentation, (2) recurring prospect and customer problems which afford clues to generalized creative approaches.

RECURRING SELLING SITUATIONS

The situations you face and the strategies you devise for meeting them will rest, of course, on what you sell and to whom. It may well be that none of the situations or the methods of dealing with them discussed below will relate directly to your circumstances. But if the examples cited stimulate your thinking in regard to the application of strategies to your particular problems, they will have achieved their end.

"I can't try them all"

One common selling problem is customer skepticism in regard to product claims. As one buyer expressed it: "Every salesman claims his line will outsell the rest. Well, I can't try them all."

I faced this situation some years ago when I was selling cocoa imported from Holland. It was used for flavoring ice cream and for making fountain syrups and hot chocolate. In the course of a day, I'd show the product to a dozen or more prospective buyers. They'd sniff it and agree that it looked good and smelled good. But then I'd get the "I can't try them all" reaction. For these buyers didn't want to change from the brands they knew. As a result, I opened only two to three new accounts a week.

Realizing that if I could find a way to break through this recurring initial resistance I'd have a winner, I concentrated on that one problem. Finally, I decided that more prospects would buy if they could taste my product in one of the final forms in which they'd be using it. So I had an attractive leather case fitted to hold eight half-pint thermos bottles. Every morning I got up early and made some wonderfully good hot chocolate with the cocoa; then I filled the thermos bottles, which I had sterilized the night before.

"May I borrow a cup?" I asked each buyer. Opening my case, I took out a thermos, removed the stopper, and poured hot chocolate into the cup—close enough to the prospect's nose so that he could appreciate the delicious aroma.

"Say, that's good," many would remark.

"That's exactly what your customers will say," I put in. "Let me send you a 100-pound drum at the barrel price; that way you can give it a real test under your conditions."

With this strategy I averaged between two and three accounts a day—a fivefold increase. One day I got eight. This increase occurred only because I awakened to the fact that taking the time to devise an answer to a problem that came up so regularly would inevitably pay off in multiple sales.

USE SAMPLES AND DEMONSTRATIONS

More important, this experience shows the close tie between problem-solving strategies and the selling tools discussed in the previous chapter. In this case it was a matter of sampling. In another one which I witnessed a demonstration did the trick.

While I was a student at Cornell University, I had an interest in a men's furnishings shop. A salesman sold us a new line of hats. On his next call, three months later, we pointed out that the new line hadn't moved very well.

"A new line isn't going to move very fast by itself," he replied. "But it will turn over if you dramatize your sales. After you have served a customer, let me make a demonstration."

Then he asked me for a mirror, which he set up in the back of the store. After I finished with the next customer, the salesman said: "Would you like to step back here? I've got something absolutely new for you to see."

Gauging the customer's proper head size, he picked out a hat in the pastel shade that he felt suited the prospect and placed it on his head, commenting briefly on some of its features. He repeated this routine with more than a dozen students who came in, and about half of those he approached wound up buying a new hat.

This demonstration of how a new line should be promoted convinced me to reverse myself and put in a good-sized order. And by following his lead we sold more new hats in one week than we normally would have sold in three months.

MAKE COMPARISONS

Another common selling problem is being squeezed out of your market by a lower-priced competing line. For instance, a lumber wholesaler who specializes in redwood found that spruce and ponderosa pine had taken a large share of the outside trim and cornice lumber market because dealers in his area believed that these species performed satisfactorily at lower costs. His redwood volume kept falling—until he stopped to work out a strategy for coping with this important recurring situation.

"I prepared a simple comparison chart," he writes, "of the dealer's true costs for the two top grades of ponderosa pine, spruce, and redwood, using factors which often fail to get consideration. With this chart I can quickly show a dealer that with redwood he can buy a superior product at a comparable price and sell it at a higher mark-up or make easier sales because of the benefits it offers his customers. Because this strategy hits directly at the main objection to redwood that my prospects raise, I find that my presentations take less time while my closing average keeps rising."

SELL A BIG IDEA: ANOTHER APPROACH TO PRICE COMPETITION

As the next example illustrates, more than one strategy can be designed to meet the same recurring situation. Thus it is important to consider the type of product you sell and the kind of customer you deal with when working out your answer to a given situation. In the previous case the salesman met price competition with a comparison chart. In the next case price competition crumbled before a "big idea" approach.

Salesmen for the Bulova Watch Company used to sell watches per se. Now they sell their dealers on the fact that Bulova can help them build a larger watch business, with a fair profit margin on each watch. "Bulova selects its dealers very carefully," the salesmen tell their prospects, "and its selective dealer policies protect your profits; its extensive line lets you concentrate on Bulova, sell more watches than before, and enjoy decent margins."

When the salesmen sold watches, people would shop the jewelers but buy at discount stores. Then Bulova developed the big idea: to sell only to jewelers who wanted to resell at a fair margin. When Bulova salesmen zeroed in on this idea, they sold more watches, and so did their customers.

Not that a big idea is absolutely essential for coping with recurring—and discouraging—price competition. Just facing up to it and thinking more clearly about your own offering can do the trick, as one salesman demonstrates.

"I have learned that a man who has only price to sell is very vulnerable to a competitor who sells quality and service. Before I thought through this recurring problem, I was inclined to stop selling when I was confronted with a lower price—as I so often was. But now I stress the quality of our products and demonstrate the prompt service we are known for. I find that orders come much easier now that I no longer fear that recurring phrase 'I can get it for less.' "

"I'll think it over": the recurring sales killer

All too often the phrase "I'll think it over" kills a sale. In many cases the salesman stops selling today in the hope of getting an order tomorrow. Sometimes this may be the best thing to do. But much more often a strategy geared to getting by this recurring roadblock will bring in sales that would otherwise be irretrievably lost. Here too more than one strategy might do the trick.

For example, if you are selling in a field with constant price changes, you can readily underscore the importance of buying now, before the market goes up. Similarly, if you are selling life insurance or other protection, you can emphasize the need for locking the barn door today.

USE SALES INDUCEMENTS

But your best bet will be to offer some tangible inducement if the prospect will do business now. An encyclopedia salesman spreads a set of his bindings on the floor. To stimulate immediate action, he spreads another free set of bindings as an inducement to the prospect who concludes the sale while the representative is there. Since the extra set represents real value, it makes a powerful persuader.

For the commercial salesman, inducers may include such things as premiums, cooperative advertising, training in the use of the product, promotional plans, and a "buy today" approach to reap the benefits now rather than later.

One of the most popular and most effective inducers is the trial or introductory order. The trial may be sweetened by offering to send the product with a return privilege. Or it may be practical to offer an introductory package with an inducement or with extra goods.

They spent too much unproductive time

By staying alert to recurring selling situations, a salesman may at times come up with an answer to a problem that has been plaguing management and his fellow salesmen as well. A paper bag manufacturer, for example, had to deal with 47 classes of retailers who ordered hundreds of sizes and styles. Accordingly, the firm's salesmen constantly faced the same situation: spending a great deal of time with prospects sorting out the many different sizes for each order. At the same time, they often had to cope with a competitor who offered a special item which they could not at the moment produce.

One salesman who saw all this unproductive time eating into his possible earnings suggested that the firm standardize its line on a smaller number of sizes and styles. After due consideration, management settled on 19 basic variations, with a chart showing which style was best for which purpose.

Because it made bag selection easier, buyers went for the idea in a big way. By funneling orders to these standardized sizes and styles, the customer got better prices and faster delivery. And the salesmen got rid of a recurring time waster, thereby paving the way to more sales.

IMPROVE THE APPLICATION OF SELLING SKILLS

If you cannot come up with a new strategy to meet a specific recurring selling situation, you can still improve matters by strengthening your selling skills. Analyze your presentation step by step. Make notes from memory after completing a call. Even better, record a typical presentation on tape. You can do this on your own, or you might ask a fellow salesman to work with you in role-playing fashion to review the presentation objectively.

ASK "WHY?"

Such reviews have pinpointed for many salesmen an important area for improving their approaches to recurring situations—that is, the need to use inquiry more consistently.

For example, a town official who had good relations with the doctors in his community bought a drug store close to the largest hospital and convenient to the offices of many of the town's physicians. The new owner planned to build the kind of store that would appeal to the doctors. To this end, he wanted to emphasize the prescription trade. Four wholesale drug houses served that town. The head of one of these firms was a good friend of the new owner. Yet the latter chose one of his friend's competitors as chief supplier.

"Why did you pick that firm?" asked the friend.

"Because its service is geared to the kind of operation I want to develop. It has a very broad line of prescription drugs. It provides motorcycle delivery in emergencies. It holds occasional seminars which would be very useful to me. And so on."

"We offer all those things!" said his friend.

"Maybe you do," said the owner, "but your representative never mentioned them. He told me only about services in which I was not especially interested.

"On the other hand, when your competitor's salesman called, he asked a lot of questions to find out what I had in mind and why. In fact, he helped crystallize my plans for developing the kind of business I wanted. Naturally, I prefer to deal with such a representative."

This story pinpoints the merit of asking why. It also highlights the importance of using the O PIB'ROC pocket card.

Here was a man who had the advantage of friendship. Yet his salesman lost out in a typical recurring situation. Instead of using inquiry to find out which services appealed to the specific prospect, the salesman presented what he thought were the main selling points.

Had he thoughtfully reviewed the card, he might well have seen the need for asking questions first, as the successful salesman did.

RECURRING PROSPECT PROBLEMS

Considering the best way of handling a recurring prospect or customer problem can be even more productive than tackling a recurring selling situation. For in the former case you are back in the realm of the creative approach.

As one highly successful insurance adjuster reports: "I have repeatedly encountered the situation of an agent training a new girl. I always try to help her, carefully explaining coverage and warning her not to commit the company to liability. Most agents appreciate this and give me additional claims to process."

Generalizing from this approach, the district manager of the insurance firm organized eight evening training sessions for claims girls in local agencies. Starting with a review of standard fire contracts and forms, the sessions covered every kind of risk the company insures.

"Whenever I run into this problem now," the adjuster writes, "I immediately suggest these sessions as a solution to training difficulties. This has become a key factor in securing new business."

This same strategy can be adapted by any salesman whose customers must resell his products. Almost always they will appreciate some help in increasing their turnover —and in many cases this may take the form of training their sales personnel to do a better job.

The salesladies weren't selling

For example, one hosiery salesman found that a major recurring customer problem was the need to get the product story across to the saleslady behind the counter. "All the quality built into the product and all our supporting promotional efforts," the salesman says, "go down the drain if the retailer cannot spark the interest and imagination of this key person."

The salesman induced management to tackle this situation by organizing a series of one-day training seminars conducted by informed and experienced saleswomen. Interested stores sent their salespeople to the seminars on a staggered basis so that everyone would gain. Participants were exposed to fashion hints, style development, proper ways of fitting customers, strategies for creating multiple sales, and the art of building a customer following.

Results? More sales, including a higher percentage of premium items; more multiple sales, such as three pairs of stockings instead of one; a greater interest in satisfying customer needs; and improved housekeeping. A similar program has now been instituted on a nationwide basis.

KNOW WHAT YOU'RE LOOKING FOR

Tackling recurring prospect problems will yield the best results with a minimum of time and effort when you know in which direction to look. As in the above case, selective training of office, store, or factory personnel can provide an important competitive edge. In many other fields the salesman can close a good percentage of extra sales by securing favorable financing.

One real estate broker, for example, knows that many of his prospects worry about down payments. So for every area he regularly covers he has prepared a list of credit sources which he immediately offers when the question of down payments comes up. This information-at-my-fingertips approach impresses prospects both with his expertise and with his readiness to help. And because this situation recurs so often, the approach has been an important factor in the impressive sales record he has built up over the years.

OFFER A PROMOTIONAL IDEA

Many firms which sell to retailers provide their salesmen with a variety of promotional plans for helping the dealers move the goods off their shelves. In addition, creative salesmen who cast a thoughtful eye on recurring customer problems often develop their own promotional ideas.

In one case a salesman for a well-known cold remedy adopted the idea of listing recurring customer problems in the order of their importance. He discovered that the one big problem his customers faced—a problem affecting his own volume—was the increasingly tough discount competition. Thinking it over in preparation for a call on a national chain, he hit on the idea of making each outlet a "cold remedy center" stocking a variety of remedies, with his own taking a featured position.

The salesman worked out a presentation emphasizing three major benefits of setting up such a department. A cold remedy center would help each outlet (1) increase store traffic, (2) become more competitive with discount stores, (3) create a one-stop store for many needs.

Using available survey data, the salesman developed figures showing the total market, the share the chain might capture, the variety of products to be stocked, how the department should be set up, and so on. To start the ball rolling, he gave one good customer who was not competitive with the chain a special deal to open the first center. Then he had photos taken showing the large number of customers shopping in the new department with its complete and attractive displays; he backed this up with a favorable letter from the store manager. In due time the chain bought the idea, which led to bigger orders and turnover for all concerned.

All this, of course, took considerable time and help from the home office. But it has since helped the salesman establish dozens of centers with no extra preparation time. He simply uses the same presentation, back-up photos, and letters of endorsement with every prospect and customer confronted with the same situation.

BUILDING THE HABIT

Building the habit of coping with recurring selling situations means sitting down and doing the job now. That is, list your recurring roadblocks and your prospects' recurring problems and arrange them in the order of priority. Then start working out a strategy to cope with the first situation.

Apply that strategy consistently whenever the recurring situation crops up. When you are comfortable with it—when you are getting better results—start working on the next one. Do this regularly, and the habit of coping with recurring situations will surely "take."

13

How to Sell Yourself:
The Art of Cultivating Sound Customer Relations

"First you've got to sell yourself."

Somewhere along the line you've probably heard a seasoned salesman express the point in exactly those words. For most representatives know that one basic difference between the top producer and the average salesman is that the former has mastered the art of cultivating sound customer relations. And in so doing he has gained the inside track on one major source of continued and growing income.

A tremendous amount of business turns upon such personal relationships, especially when the products and prices of competing firms are essentially the same. Indeed, in some cases competitors have actually offered greater benefits at lower prices, only to see the order go to the salesman who sold himself to best advantage. And in other cases buyers have awarded business to salesmen who have sold themselves effectively, without even waiting for a competitive offer.

Sure, you know all this. But it's a good bet that you have never been trained to sell yourself in an organized manner. Like most salesmen, you have undoubtedly built closer relationships by picking up the tab for lunch or drinks, buying tickets for a show, talking about matters close to the client's heart, and the like.

While such things do play a part, selling yourself goes much deeper than the personal touch alone. For the most part you can build or improve upon your customer relationships—making them more profitable as well as more enduring—by focusing on the following areas:

> Build on a firm foundation.
> Win the customer's confidence.
> Help them keep you in mind.
> Remember the personal touch.

BUILD ON A FIRM FOUNDATION

Selling yourself has sometimes been treated, rather misleadingly, in terms of personality. Thus we get the popular picture of the "personality kid" whose charm and enthusiasm make all and sundry rush to sign on the dotted line.

Actually, few successful salesmen can be fitted into any preconceived personality pattern. As Carl Hoffman, partner in McKinsey & Company, says: "We must throw out the notion that the good salesman conforms to some ideal 'personality profile.' *Anyone can sell himself and his products if he treats the customer as a man with a problem to be solved—not as someone to be manipulated into a sale."*

Hoffman's words strikingly echo the theme of the chapter on creative selling. For there we saw that the *constructive call,* designed precisely to help the "man with a problem to be solved," puts you into the most favorable position for your selling interview. It beats out personality; it often beats out price; and on occasion it beats out friendship too.

Ideas are the buyer's best friend

Not that friendship will hurt. It's just that you won't normally build volume on friendship alone. For that word takes on a different meaning during business hours.

As the director of purchasing of the Allied Chemical Corporation sums it up: "The salesman who calls with some useful idea in his head is the buyer's best friend."

A pleasant smile coupled with a genuine interest in people will inspire friendly relationships. But they'll go much deeper from a selling standpoint when they rest upon a solid foundation of constructive ideas.

Several years ago August Richter, who sells industrial equipment, took over an account from a fellow salesman who was moving out to the West Coast. This man explained that he supplied about 30 percent of the customer's requirements only because he and the buyer were personal friends. Let August tell the rest of the story.

"I figured if that was as far as he could go on friendship, I'd better have something more meaningful going for me. After all, I had never even met the buyer.

"Before making my first call, I looked into the situation pretty carefully. The plant was in a town about 60 miles from our offices, so the customer always had trouble getting parts for emergency jobs—from us and from his other suppliers. There was always a phone call, plus transportation expenses, which had to be added to the bill.

"When I came in for my initial order, I outlined my idea. I suggested installing bins in the plant's supply room and labeling them by part name and number of parts to be kept on hand. On every subsequent call I inventoried those parts and worked out replacement orders as necessary. The emergency flaps, the extra time, and the extra expenditures all evaporated.

"Practically overnight I gained a friendly respect from this buyer. Ever since that time, I have made it a point to bring in a new idea on every other call at least. One time it might do with applications, another time with maintenance. Today my volume from this account is nearly twice as great as the previous salesman's, which was built up on friendship alone."

Ideas are indeed a buyer's best friend.

The idea doesn't have to relate

The ideas that August develops when cultivating good relations tend to be connected to his products. But this need not be the case. What counts is the habit of selling yourself by constructive means.

Consider the case of a bank officer who was cultivating the account of a very large laundry. The customer showed a net profit percentage well above the average for the industry. Obviously, here was an account which could be valuable, given careful cultivation. To this end, the officer sought a way to get closer to the customer on a personal level.

The firm had recently opened a coin laundry across town from its home office and plant. If successful, it was to be the forerunner of a chain of automatic laundries—which would surely open up interesting financing possibilities.

Several days before his first appointment with the principals, the banker dropped in at the coin laundry. A discussion with the attendant disclosed that business was on the slow side, even though no laundries of any kind were available in the general neighborhood. And there was only one dry-cleaning outlet, located in a tailor shop two blocks away.

These facts gave the officer his idea. When he called at the home office, the principals confirmed the fact that the coin laundry was slow in developing volume. The banker asked: "Do you think it might help to use the place also as a receiving station for general laundry and dry cleaning which could be done here at the main plant?"

"Now that's an idea I should have thought of myself," the president exclaimed. He called in an assistant, and they talked about it briefly. The assistant was then asked to put the idea to work.

The principals were now in a receptive mood for the officer's suggestion that they open an account. One said: "I really must give consideration to a banker who thinks as constructively about our business as you do." Clearly, he was sold on the banker personally. But note that the idea related to "our business," not the banker's.

This means that any salesman who had dealings with that customer could have sold himself with the same idea— had he thought of it first. He might have been selling laundry equipment; he might have been offering business insurance. Whatever he was selling, his way would have been better paved with helpful ideas.

Turn on the charm if you will; flash that smile; toss in a

cheery hello. But if you want a profitable business relationship, sell yourself with ideas.

WIN THE CUSTOMER'S CONFIDENCE

You can best gain your customer's confidence by demonstrating your sincere concern for his welfare. Taking pains to come in with helpful ideas is the first step in this direction. You can complete the job most effectively in two ways: (1) be dependable, (2) keep the customer informed.

BE DEPENDABLE

Here we see a natural overlap with the techniques of follow-through. When you make good on your promises of performance and servicing, you have surely sold the client on your dependability.

"Don't oversell"

But now we go beyond that. Winning your customer's confidence starts with being realistic about everything you say. Above all, it means promising only what you can deliver.

Though confidence is built slowly, it can be shattered quickly. Let your client once feel that you are solving your problems at his expense, and your personal image can be smashed for good.

Say, for example, that you haven't been closing many sales in a given period. The pressure is on for you to produce.

In such circumstances you can easily be tempted to oversell: to talk the unwary customer into a deal he doesn't really need. Then up goes automatic sales resistance on every subsequent call. Maybe you bail yourself out—and maybe not.

I remember a moment I spent with a salesman who was on his way to an appointment. His boss had told me the man was one of the most consistent big money earners in his field.

"I can only give you a couple of minutes," this man said when I approached him.

"Suppose I joined your organization as a salesman," I said. "What one thing would help me build a regular following?"

Without a moment's hesitation he replied: "Don't oversell."

"Can you elaborate on that point in the minute or so you've got left?"

"I have about 70 regular customers," he told me. "I got started with at least a third of them *because some other salesman oversold them*—for example, by indicating specific benefits or features which did not fully materialize.

"I have never deliberately oversold. Sometimes I have consciously undersold when a customer inquired about shipments I knew he didn't need. The people I deal with know they can count on what I tell them. And I can count on them."

In the course of several interviews, the customer will spot such integrity. And most customers will stick with the man who displays it.

"They can count on me"

A representative who deals in office systems equipment tells how selling personal dependability has contributed to the profitable repeat business he has built up over the years. As he puts it: "Our customers have learned that they can count on me to come around and make sure everything works out successfully. I consider this as much a part of my job as getting the order.

"Usually, my equipment represents a change in the procedures of the customer. Many of the people who have to do the actual work get mixed up for a while. I try to make it easy for them by making myself available to help them over the hurdles. This can mean going in and working with clerks, bookkeepers, secretaries, and other people until they feel at home with the equipment.

"Naturally, this makes me pretty much 'part of the family' in the company. And you'd be surprised how much influence a secretary can wield when it comes to deciding what office equipment to buy."

KEEP THE CUSTOMER INFORMED

William Appleby has earned a reputation for reliability by leveling with his customers immediately if anything goes wrong. He cites a typical example.

"We ran into a five-week delay on one tough order last year because of spring road break-up. Because I was frank with the customer and advised him that the shipment would be late, he cooperated extremely well. He bought just enough material from a local supplier for his immediate needs, but with the understanding that we would complete the shipment as soon as we could get through.

"Had I not kept him informed, he would probably have bought the whole order from a local man, charging the difference to our account. And he might well have started using that source regularly. This reputation for giving my customers the real score at all times has gained me much extra business over the years."

Help Them Keep You in Mind

Every salesman has to have his customers keep him in mind even though he may be out of sight. The mails are clogged with calendars, for instance, come the year's end. And blotters with advertising clutter up many a desk.

Here again, your reminders will pay extra dividends when you work at making them different—and useful.

Calendars with a twist

One successful salesman out West deals with oil companies. Every year he sends his customers—and some prospects as well—two wall maps. Each has a calendar, but they also show clearly the current oil situation in the customer's area. Of course, they bear the salesman's name and carry an advertising plug.

These maps are so good that they have become almost essential to many of his clients. When a dealer comes into the buyer's office to discuss a possible lease, he is asked to pinpoint the area on the wall maps. The buyer can immediately tell if his firm would be interested or if further discussion would be a waste of time.

USE YOUR IMAGINATION

True, those maps are quite expensive. But a constructive reminder need not entail an appreciable outlay to solidify customer relations. What it takes is a knowledge of client needs wedded to a modicum of imagination.

In one case, for example, a simple chart outlining the various uses of a line of lubricants boosted one man from back-up position to favored supplier. Another man has a wide collection of simple but practical reminders, ranging from technical bulletins to slide rules. "That way I can vary my reminders," he says, "leaving a different one on each visit."

When reading an article which may be of interest to their customers and prospects, some salesmen will clip it, make copies, and send them out. One man makes them different by circling the item with thick black crayon and writing a note to the customer in red: "Pete, thought you'd be interested." Then he signs his name. That's all—but it stands out and is remembered.

KEEP IT PRACTICAL

Even when you can't think of something different, reminders of a practical nature will still stand out. As one salesman writes: "When trying to build good relations with new prospects or inactive customers, I find the best kind of reminder for my purposes is literature with end-use or application ideas geared to their operations. Sometimes I'll just leave a memo sheet outlining a promotion idea.

"Of course, I always have my name and firm name on each item I leave. And I get a surprising number of orders phoned in on the strength of these reminders."

REMEMBER THE PERSONAL TOUCH

Once you've laid the proper foundation, gained the customer's confidence, and helped him keep you in mind, you've crossed the biggest selling-yourself hurdle. Beyond that, a genuine interest in your customer as a person—his family, his hobbies, his health—imparts a warmth which adds the overtones of friendship to what is essentially a business relationship.

DO IT NATURALLY

As one representative points out, the best way to be friendly is not to pretend but to take an active interest in the things that mean a lot to both you and your customer.

He writes: "How I do it depends on the customer. In some cases, I'll talk about his hobby with real enthusiasm because it's my hobby too. If it isn't, I don't get deeply involved.

"Or I'll compare notes on his grandchildren and mine because we both get a kick out of our kids and their families."

Of course, there are no general rules for making friends and getting customers to like you. Some salesmen can pick up a tab and make it a gesture of friendship rather than of business. The main thing is to do it in a natural way.

If you've got to force it, forget it; the artificiality will seep through, and the effect may be negative.

BE DIFFERENT

Most salesmen do a good job on the personal side of customer relations. Yet here too, when you do it thoughtfully, spicing your personal gesture with a touch of imagination, the impact is all the greater.

One man makes his social contacts different by avoiding the routine. "My rule on the personal side is to show my interest with small, sentimental touches that are different from the usual. For example, I don't send Christmas cards. Instead, I keep a customer file which tells me at a glance whose birthday or wedding anniversary is on tap so that I can send an appropriate card. Or if someone in the family is sick, I always send flowers. Such small touches, in my experience, lend a warmth which you can't buy with more elaborate kinds of entertainment or with the more usual seasonal remembrances."

That extra bit of imagination has added up over the years to an appreciable number of truly friendly relationships, and extra sales have been a natural outcome.

Flowers—or a birthday cake?

One salesman was all set to send flowers to a customer who was celebrating his twenty-fifth anniversary in business. But when he envisioned the profusion of flowers that would be descending on the customer, he had second thoughts.

In place of flowers, he sent a big, inscribed birthday cake. Everybody at the party tasted the cake and knew where it came from. When the story of the anniversary appeared in the local press, the cake and donor were mentioned.

What happened to those who gave flowers? They each received an identical note of appreciation. But the salesman who had transcended routine received warm personal thanks for his thoughtfulness from the members of the firm.

It was just the book he wanted

Here is a case in which I was the salesman. I had a prospect for a program to help officers sell their bank's services more creatively. My prospect was deeply involved in community affairs and was a forward-looking banker. Because I was very busy at the time, I had only been able to make one call; however, a competitor had made a number of calls, including several luncheons.

Thinking the problem over, I recalled an inspiring book I had read which echoed the forward-looking philosophy of my prospect. So I sent him a copy, inscribing the flyleaf with a remark that here was a thinker who shared many of his ideas.

A few days later, my prospect started reading the book. He was so intrigued that he kept at it for a good part of the night. Who was he thinking of the next morning? You guessed it—he phoned me and suggested I call.

Yes, I got the assignment, and I'm convinced that it pays to be different.

BE HELPFUL AND FRIENDLY

But remember, while imagination helps, in the long run selling yourself turns on a very simple formula: be helpful; be friendly. On one of my sales consulting assignments I went into the field with a refrigeration and air-conditioning salesman for a wholesale organization. During the couple of days we spent together, every customer we met greeted him warmly.

Why? Because that salesman constantly demonstrated a personal interest in his customers, going out of his way to be helpful and friendly. He would go all out to locate difficult-to-find items; he'd get emergency parts to dealers or contractors in a hurry when they were desperately needed. And he always had a friendly word: an interested query about wives and children, a warm smile, and a cheery hello.

This was not a one-way street. Many of these dealers had their inquiries well organized for his arrival; orders for many items were prepared and waiting so that he would lose as little time as possible. The wife of one dealer had baked a cake for the salesman to take home to his wife and family.

These buyers obviously liked the salesman, and equally obviously he liked them. Not surprisingly, this man is the top producer among the 17 salesmen in his organization, even though his territory has less potential volume than the average.

BUILDING THE HABIT

How can you sell yourself effectively? By doing *consistently* what most of us do only to a degree. Above all, this means following an organized program designed to build the habit of cultivating good customer relations. Start now. List every major customer and prospect. Then consider the following points:

1. Have you always looked for and taken the extra step of being helpful—the step that brings you closer to the customer and puts you ahead of your competitors?

2. Do you follow through on every promise concerning quality, delivery, and availability of stock? Do you avoid overselling? If not, make a point of being especially cautious in these areas in the future.

3. Are the reminders you leave with your customers and prospects useful and imaginative enough to stand out in their minds?

4. Have you been friendly and warm in your contacts without being artificial or overly aggressive?

Building the habit of selling yourself means winning the customer's confidence every step of the way. Always remember:

Do it in a way that reflects *your* personality.
Do it thoughtfully, with a dash of imagination.
Build it on the bedrock of constructive help.

14

How to Manage
Your Time Effectively

According to an extensive McGraw-Hill study, the typical salesman spends only 40 percent of his working time with customers and prospects. Indeed, many experienced sales managers say this overstates the case because it doesn't take waiting time into account.

For example, the sales manager of one major corporation estimates actual face-to-face selling time at only two hours a day, or less than 500 hours a year. For the salesman who earns $15,000 and has expenses of $5,000, the value of each selling hour comes to over $40.

While these figures may vary from man to man, one thing remains constant. Sound time management can spell the difference between outstanding and mediocre performance. To achieve competence in this area, center your thoughts around two broad headings: (1) make your selling time more productive, (2) squeeze more selling hours out of your working day.

MAKE YOUR SELLING TIME MORE PRODUCTIVE

When he contemplates all the things he must do to make his calls effective and then considers the limited time at his disposal, many a salesman has fervently wished for a 26-hour day. If you can't make the day longer, you can make it more productive.

How? You can spend more of your time where it counts the most. You can walk into each interview better prepared to make your sale. You can allot more time to prospecting and development selling.

SPEND YOUR TIME WHERE IT COUNTS THE MOST

To get the highest possible yield out of every selling hour, you must invest your time where the potential for sales and earnings is greatest. Most salesmen have more customers and prospects than they can effectively cultivate. And all too often they burn up shoe leather attempting to give equal coverage to every account when they could be spending more time with the more productive ones.

For while some customers are regular buyers of substantial volume, others buy less frequently and in smaller amounts. And while the former may be converted to customers quickly, the latter may require too much time in relation to their sales potential.

As studies have shown, as many as four-fifths of a representative's sales are made to as few as one-fifth of his customers. Indeed, one study of wholesale drug salesmen revealed that those who were making the fewest calls per day were recording the largest volume of sales.

Why? Because these men were following a calling plan based on carefully calculated productivity estimates. By devoting more time to the better prospects, they were closing more sales.

It comes down to this: to cultivate your territory most productively, you must emphasize the quality of your calls rather than the quantity.

DEVELOP A CREAM-SEPARATING DEVICE

There are several ways of planning the best use of your time. One of the simplest is to identify each account and prospect in accordance with its present importance and future potential. Then schedule your calling frequency accordingly.

Every salesman does this to some degree. But in my experience those who adopt a formal cream-separating device boost their sales volume higher and faster than those who do it haphazardly.

He makes fewer calls, but better ones

Gene Ruppert, one of the top producers of an office systems organization, draws up a master rating and frequency schedule every year. He begins by placing his customers and prospects into high-, medium-, or low-dollar-volume categories on the basis of actual records and his knowledge of the field. Then he balances the time he spent with each account over the year against the actual or anticipated results.

Weighing these factors—present customer volume, customer and prospect potential, and invested selling time—according to values determined by his cost and profitability circumstances, he pinpoints the overall amount of time he will spend on a given account for the coming year.

In grading an account, Gene emphasizes potential as well as current volume. Thus a low-volume customer (or even a nonbuyer) with heavy volume and profit potential may be rated higher than a heavy-volume buyer whose business is on the decline.

Once the ratings have been settled to Gene's satisfaction, each account is slotted into a corresponding calling schedule. That is, the A accounts are called upon once a week, the B accounts every two weeks, the C accounts once a month.

Originally, Gene had established a D category to be called on quarterly. But an analysis of his time inventory convinced him that he could not hope to follow through on his proposed schedule and still maintain the desired quality of presentations. This left him with an important policy decision.

Should he lengthen the time between calls? Or should he cut out certain customers and prospects?

Gene decided to eliminate the marginal accounts and focus on the most productive ones. That is, he held to an ABC schedule, cutting out all D customers and prospects.

In the five years since he hooked on to this cream-separating device, Gene's volume and earnings have moved up steadily. He credits the increase in large measure to the practice of concentrating his time where it counts the most.

HANDLING THE MARGINAL ACCOUNT

Whatever rating system you use, determining the proper classification requires careful analysis and judgment. For cream separating isn't always a simple matter.

The relatively small but consistent volume from a regular buyer, for example, may add up over the years to much more profit and earnings than a big one-shot sale. And careful cultivation may be the necessary prelude to converting a no-volume prospect to a heavy-volume customer.

While you can get some help from your manager, the classification must fit your situation and square with your judgment, for you are the man who manages the territory. However you do it, you will eventually come down to the marginal accounts, those which pose the inevitable dilemma: "Should I keep them or dump them?"

In the example above, Gene Ruppert sloughed off his D customers and prospects because the cost of cultivating their business—in terms of excess time investment—was too high. Yet many of the marginal accounts of yesterday are today's biggest-volume outlets. Since you can't always measure their growth potential accurately, it pays to find a way of maintaining contact with some marginal accounts without eating too deeply into your precious selling time.

To this end, some salesmen establish a special "telephone contact" category for certain marginal prospects who can be called as fill-ins when regularly scheduled calls must be canceled. Again, whether or not it pays to maintain even such minimal contact with marginal prospects and customers depends upon your own circumstances and judgment.

REVIEW AND REVISE

Of course, you can never do a perfect job of cream separating. For as conditions change, categories change. The A account of today may be the C account of tomorrow —and vice versa. So review and revise your customer and prospect list from time to time in the light of new information and new experience.

As one man writes: "Since time is money and time is limited, I reclassify my customers quarterly. Both their sales potential and mine are estimated in making the original classifications and revisions. On a quarterly basis only a few changes need to be made—but each one adds up in time saved and money earned."

CREAM SEPARATING BY TERRITORY

A number of salesmen report good results from cream separating by sales areas as well as by individual customers. First they evaluate different parts of their territories by sales potential, often with the help of management. Then they determine how intensively they will cultivate each part.

Frank Walker tells an interesting story of how it worked for him. "Some time ago," he says, "my firm had a sales consultant go out into the field with me. I started beefing to him about my territory being too small. 'I can't find enough decent prospects,' I insisted. The man said nothing to this, but I noticed him clocking my calls for the rest of the day.

"After dinner that night, he finally took up the point. 'Frank,' he said, 'the way I worked it out, you don't spend enough time with each prospect to do a really good job on him. Look,' he went on, 'here's a local road map. Would you spot your present buyers and prospects on this map?'

"When I finished, he showed me how these clustered in certain areas, with a few buyers sprinkled here and there by themselves. Then he said something that really rocked me. 'If you cut your territory instead of extending it, and concentrate your calls where you have the heaviest grouping of customers and prospects, you'll get the additional business you've been wanting.'

"Well, I didn't go for it right away, but it kept working on my mind. Finally, I figured I had little to lose by trying it. First I picked seven areas where I had the heaviest groupings. Then, checking back over my records, I listed them according to profitability. I also considered such factors as servicing costs and travel time before I stabilized the listings.

"By cutting my territory down to size and allocating my time to each area according to profitability, I was able to devote myself to more important customers and prospects. And by allotting enough time to those who were small on the books but big in potential, I found I could actually realize that potential in a fair percentage of cases."

TALK TO THE RIGHT MAN

Any salesman who has been in the field for any length of time will agree that he spends too much time with people who lack the power of decision and who can do little to further the sale.

True, you must often cultivate many people who can be helpful even though they can't decide. These "assistants" may range upon occasion from secretaries and telephone operators to executive vice presidents.

For all that, when you fail to find out who the decision makers are and get to them reasonably soon, you lose precious time and often sales as well.

Whether you are selling to business firms or to individuals, the trick is to work up a checklist of questions to help you determine the right person or persons to deal with. For example: "Who has the authority to buy?" "Will the man I am seeing have to consult with others before buying?" "Will the decision to buy in this case be a group decision?" "Is there reason to suspect that there is a silent partner who must be consulted?"

In addition, take every opportunity to ask questions of those who have some knowledge of the inside workings. These include secretaries, telephone operators, junior executives, and customers of the firm.

"Who besides yourself would be consulted in deciding upon my line?" is a question which will often bring helpful information. Getting to the right person helps you invest your time where it counts the most.

PAVE THE WAY IN ADVANCE

The likelihood of meeting with the right persons is usually increased by making appointments in advance. One day Lester Goodell, who sells air-conditioning equipment, phoned Alan Granson, the head of a secretarial school. "Mr. Granson," he said, "my name is Lester Goodell. I represent Jenkins & Company; we specialize in office air-conditioning installations.

"Now, as I understand it, your business generally slows down considerably during the hot summer months. Is that right, Mr. Granson?"

"That's true. Frankly, we don't always feel like putting in a full week ourselves at that time of year."

"I know what you mean. But have you ever considered that you might beat the seasonal slump—at least to some extent—by installing equipment that squeezed the moisture out of the air while keeping the temperature down? And I'm sure that you and your teachers and your pupils would find it much easier to put in a good day's work."

"We have two offices and six classrooms. Roughly what kind of money are you talking about?"

"That depends on the sun exposure of your rooms and how many cubic feet you must keep under controlled temperatures during the hot, damp days of summer. If I could see you next Thursday or Friday, I could measure your space and talk over your needs. That's the only way we can design an installation that will keep your rooms comfortable at a reasonable cost."

"I'm all tied up on Thursday. How about making it 2:30 next Friday?"

"Thank you. I'll be there. May I ask if there is anyone else in your organization who could be helpful if he sat in on the discussion?"

"One of my teachers is a part owner of the school. He knows more about this kind of thing than I do. I'll ask him to sit in."

"Very good, Mr. Granson. I'll look forward to meeting him too."

Had Lester Goodell not paved the way, the partner might very well have heard his story secondhand and, not getting it fully, would more likely have objected to the adoption of the air-conditioning project. As it was, Lester had the decision makers present and consummated his sale.

GO IN PREPARED

Al Sears, former marketing vice president of Remington Rand, makes an addition to the "right man" situation.

"You should know not only whom you are going to see but what things are important to him: price, performance, brand name, service, engineering, and so on.

"The time to make your first report on your prospect," he adds, "is before you make your first call. That way you can get right to the point *without wasting your time or his.*" I've been out with a number of salesmen who keep a folder in their cars containing a record of each customer or prospect on whom they plan to call. It includes copies of invoices, names of personnel, comments of value, and the best times for calling. They review the folder in planning their calls or before going in. Sometimes they take it with them for ready reference.

CONSIDER DEVELOPMENT AND MAINTENANCE CALLS

With many lines the development of new accounts requires intensive cultivation. But after the account is producing a good volume of business, you may not need to spend so much time to maintain the account adequately. Accounts will always need attention, lest competitors edge their way in. In some instances, however, you can make fewer calls but still keep in touch regularly by phone.

ALLOT MORE TIME TO PROSPECTING

"You are not managing your time to greatest effect unless you allow a minimum of 20 percent for prospecting," says the sales manager of one large corporation. He points out that "you are most productive as a salesman only when you are actively opening new accounts, cultivating new prospects, and increasing your share of existing markets. The more you can logically maximize this part of your selling time, the more you and the company will gain."

This brings us to the second phase of effective time management.

SQUEEZE MORE SELLING HOURS OUT OF YOUR WORKING DAY

Recently I helped a friend make a time analysis of a large sale. When we averaged his commission against his record of time spent in swinging the deal, it turned out that he had earned $40 for each hour devoted directly or indirectly to that sale.

"But my average sale pays me over $100 an hour," he exclaimed. "I must have been nuts to spend so much time on this one."

"No, Jim, I don't think so," I said. "You see, you forget the hours behind your $100-an-hour average sale. Do you figure in the hours engaged in prospecting, planning, travel, desk time—and maybe a few long 'entertainment lunches' too?"

Jim's reaction illustrates how important it is to have a reasonably accurate account of the amount of time spent on different aspects of your job—from organizing your desk to waiting for your prospect to see you or get to the phone. And there's more involved than simply averaging your hourly income per sale.

As a salesman, your actual selling time—face to face or on the phone—represents your major working capital. Like all capital, it should be conserved, built up when possible, and invested wisely.

Good time management means *squeezing more selling hours* out of your working day while paring to the bone time invested in other directions. Sufficient time must also

be allocated to direct supporting activities: reading and research, preparing constructive presentations, prospecting,
and the like. But a well-planned time budget makes provision for these in ways that leave your actual selling-time
capital virtually intact.

Some activities may represent a pure waste of that capital—travel and waiting time, to mention two of the most
obvious ones. While such time drains cannot be lopped off
completely, they can be cut down to size.

PREPARE A TIME BUDGET

A survey of 255 salesmen in 19 different fields shows
that on the average a salesman's working day breaks down
as follows:

Getting ready to sell: planning, gathering information, prospecting	1.7 hours
Traveling, waiting time, lunch	4.2
Record keeping and other paper work	0.7
Actual selling (interviews)	2.7
Total	9.3 hours

One salesman who studied these findings couldn't believe the figures applied to him. "But after running a time
check on myself for two weeks," he says, "I was amazed to
find I was averaging only a little more than two hours a
day talking to prospects. That bothered me. So yesterday
I got down to planning my day, and I figured a number of
ways of adding more actual selling time to the day's
schedule."

The moral is clear. Before you can squeeze more selling
hours out of your working day, you must first become time-
conscious.

KEEP A TIME RECORD

How much time do you spend in the office during selling hours? How much of it is essential to your work? Do your lunch and coffee breaks cut significantly into prime selling time? Are you using a considerable amount of prime time on nonselling activities that could be reduced or eliminated?

The only way to find out where your time goes and how it might be more productively budgeted is to keep a formal time chart for a week or two. With your figures in hand, you can better allocate your "time capital" expenditures, maximizing your selling and selling support activities and cutting down sharply on the time wasters.

This analysis need not be complicated. Start on a Monday. Jot down in a notebook everything you do each working day from start to finish.

Put down the time you get into the field or pick up your phone for the first call. Note the time devoted to traveling, waiting, preparing, reading, interviewing, prospecting. Show when and how long you have lunch, how many coffee breaks you take and how long they last, how much time you put into record keeping.

Remember: this record is for *you;* if you shave your time-wasting figures, you're only cheating yourself.

At the end of the week or two of record keeping you need only make some simple arithmetic calculations. Once you have your actual time expenditures charted, you are ready to draw up a time budget that will do the best job for you. Additional suggestions on this will present themselves later in this section.

DEVELOP A TIME CONTROL PLAN

Your time budget is as good as your follow-through. And as in all budgeting, follow-through depends on planned controls.

The $25,000 idea

Finding a salesman who doesn't plan the use of his time to some extent would be a pretty hopeless job. The point is: How well does he do it—and how consistently?

When Charles Schwab headed the Bethlehem Steel Corporation, he granted an interview to the famed public relations consultant Ivy Lee. "We have more things that should be done every day," said Schwab, "than either I or my staff can ever get to. What we need is not more new ideas but more doing of what we already know.

"Show me a way to do these things in less time," Schwab continued. "If it works, I'll pay anything within reason that you bill me for."

After thinking this over, Lee replied: "I have a method that will increase your personal management efficiency— and that of everyone else who applies it—by as much as 50 percent."

Handing Schwab a blank piece of paper, he said: "Write down the most important things you must do tomorrow."

That took Schwab about five minutes.

"Now number them in the order of their true importance to you and to the firm."

This took somewhat longer: Schwab wanted to be sure he had it right.

"Okay," said Lee. "You're all set. First thing in the

morning look at item 1. Start working on it—*and stay with it until it's done.* That way, you'll do it in the least possible time.

"Then take on item 2; when that's finished, move on to item 3; and so on down the line. If you can't finish every item on your list, don't worry about it. For there's no other way you could.

"Those that are truly important you can reschedule for the next day, moving them up the line. Those that are not, you can forget about completely.

"But with this method, the things that get done are those which have the greatest real value for you and your company. Do this every working day; have your men do it too. Try it as long as you like. Then send me your check for whatever you think the idea is worth."

After two months, Charles Schwab sent Ivy Lee a $25,000 check for this time control plan. Many years later, he wrote: "That was the most profitable $25,000 I spent in my entire business career."

You can try it for nothing.

Says one man who did: "The best thing that happened was that I eliminated many chores I found weren't necessary at all. This gave me more time for the things that matter most to me: making more calls, doing more prospecting, keeping on top of market trends."

MAKE A PLAN AND CARRY IT THROUGH

Your time control plan must be *yours:* designed to fit your needs, your temperament, your schedule. Make the plan modest enough so that you can carry it through practically—but make it!

Most important, *make it a habit.* No matter how much or how little time you allocate for preparing your travel and routing schedules or setting up fill-in activities, set aside a definite day or definite hour for each task and form the habit of following through at that time come hell or high water.

What counts is regularity. Adding a little more preparation every day or every week mounts up in terms of extra sales.

PLAN YOUR TRAVEL AND ROUTING SCHEDULES

Better travel-time management can increase your active selling time *with no increase in working hours.*

Consider. A Carnegie Institute study revealed that 60 percent of a salesman's time is taken up in getting from one prospect to another and in waiting in reception rooms.

No matter how large or small your territory, you can save travel time by investing a few minutes in planning your route. Just two steps need be followed.

1. Concentrate your calls in the morning and again in the afternoon. Some salesmen build their schedules around key calls or interviews. On any given day your calling schedule will include one or more individuals or firms that you especially want to see. They may be new leads; they may have granted you definite appointments; they may be ready for closing interviews.

Following this routing method, locate your key calls on a street or road map. Then build two calling groups around them—one for the morning, one for the afternoon.

One representative says: "The grouping method gives me a good idea of where I'll be at lunch time. That way I can often arrange to have lunch with an important prospect or customer. Scheduling such lunches in advance, after I make my routing plans for the week, has helped me bring in a number of important sales."

2. Eliminate backtracking and traffic jams. Strive for the most favorable routing by eliminating or minimizing backtracking. The shorter the distance between calls and the less crisscrossing and backtracking you must do, the more stops you can make. At the same time, work out your travel schedules to avoid getting stuck in rush-hour traffic jams.

PREPARE A PLANS BOOK

Some salesmen have maximized their selling and prospecting time by working out a plans book. Here's how the representatives of one major firm do it.

Each man has an $8\frac{1}{2}'' \times 11''$ loose-leaf binder with one page for each town or section of a city; the pages are inserted according to the normal routing. At the top of each page the salesman lists his customers in that area, and at the bottom, his prospects. Alongside each name, in a series of 52 narrow columns, the salesman enters the date of each call he made that week and notes by symbol what he did— products presented, sales made, complaints or adjustments, and so on. In a cream-separating column the salesman rates each account as A, B, C, or D, where each letter represents the frequency of sales calls.

Thus the salesman has at his fingertips all the information he needs to schedule his calls to make sure that his time and effort will yield the greatest return. He may have to make another call in a different section of his territory in the afternoon. Turning to that page, he can readily develop a schedule for his afternoon calls.

With such an approach he can perhaps get from the first area to the second area on his lunch hour. If during the day he phones his office and learns that he must make an emergency call, he is once more in a position to re-arrange his routing in a few minutes. This combined cream-separating and routing book has meant more sales and earnings for every man. For the plans book not only makes more selling time available; it also increases the number of quality calls.

PLAN FILL-IN ACTIVITIES BEFOREHAND

Some prospects or customers will always be unavailable for one reason or another. Too often this makes for unproductive time gaps only because no alternative plans were drawn up in advance.

The salesman who has planned ahead can fill in such gaps by transacting business with out-of-the-way customers by telephone, phoning ahead for appointments, making new prospecting contacts, catching up on his paper work or reading, and so on. All it takes is an extra five or ten minutes of thought about the morrow before you turn in for the night.

PUT A CEILING ON WAITING TIME

Much of your selling time may be consumed in waiting to see the prospect or customer. And sometimes the waiting ends in a complete loss: you don't get to see the busy prospect anyhow.

Can this dead time be slashed?

Some salesmen have found it to their advantage to limit their waiting time drastically, putting a ceiling of 20 or 30 minutes on reception room time. When the time is up, they may request an interview at a later hour or another day. Many buyers who are held up by other work will welcome the easing of time pressure on the day's activities. Often they will make up for the delay with a warmer welcome the next time you call.

MAKE YOUR WAITING TIME MORE PRODUCTIVE

Whatever limits you place on it, *your waiting time need not be dead time.* You can conserve time during the interview by reviewing your presentation in the waiting room and arranging your materials more conveniently. You can plan ahead for your next call, work on memoranda or reports, or put in some essential reading.

Some salesmen convert waiting time to exploratory time by talking to secretaries, assistants, salespeople, and others. That way they fill out their customer file, learning more about the prospect's needs and interests.

USE THE APPOINTMENT METHOD

Many salesmen could squeeze more selling time out of the day by making more appointments. And when you have a definite appointment, the customer or prospect is usually better prepared to digest your story. He may well have given thought to the impending interview and may have asked others who can be helpful to sit in. And the chances are that his secretary will be ready to show you in with little or no delay.

With one or two appointments set up in a neighborhood, you can check your plans book for other worthwhile calls which can be made should you complete your arranged interviews faster than anticipated.

SLEEP WHERE YOU'LL WORK

When you sleep in the town where you're going to be working, you can be sure of getting started the next morning with the least possible loss of time. What's more, you can often pick up valuable information on customers and prospects from a number of local sources.

Hotel clerks often amass a surprising store of information about local people—and they're not too chary about divulging it either. With no expense and no loss of selling time, you can pick up facts that can help you reach the best prospects in town.

One of the most successful salesmen of mutual funds, who works out of Denver, drives up to the local gas station the evening before, fills up with gas, and asks: "Who's making good money in this town?"

Corny? To be sure—but it works!

And don't overlook the possibilities of the local press. Andy Bellows, who sells business insurance in a couple of Southern states, makes a point of reading the local paper after he checks in at his motel. That way he picks up both leads and ideas that personalize his presentation.

"Staring right at me one evening on the front page was an account of an accident at a large warehouse," Andy says. "It seems that several men had been hurt when the 1,200-pound bales they were handling toppled over. From the motel clerk I learned that there had been other such accidents.

"Here was a selling situation for me. For one thing, the warehouse needed good coverage. For another, some safety measures would be helpful to it. I used the latter point to establish a good rapport with the warehouse managers.

"For when I called and introduced myself, I didn't talk insurance right away. Instead, I referred to the accident I had read about and asked the managers if they thought that fork lifts would almost completely eliminate the safety hazard in handling those heavy bales and cut down their insurance rates. I also asked if the fork lifts wouldn't increase the speed and efficiency of their warehouse crews.

"Well, let me tell you, they were really impressed by my interest in their problems and by my knowledge of warehouse workings. The story that I read in the evening paper wound up as a sale for me.

"Nor was this the first time. I've found that when I sleep where I'll be working, I frequently pick up data which I can use when I'm making calls."

HAVE A COMPLETE PLAN FOR EACH DAY

Staying where you work will help you know, at the latest by the night before, what customers and prospects you will visit on the morrow, what you will offer each one, and how you will present the benefits to him. Make sure your list of customers and prospects for the day is long enough so that you will not run out of calls should an unusual number of prospects be unavailable.

One of the most successful salesmen I know has developed the habit of mentally making each call the evening before. "I can usually do it in an hour or less," he says, "since a number of my approaches and offerings are quite similar. But when I occasionally fail to do it, my sales record suffers."

RATIONALIZE YOUR PAPER WORK

Some salesmen make their daily call reports as they go along, using their waiting time as suggested above. But in most cases too much paper work piles up, getting in the way of more productive activities.

To cut down on paper work, analyze each item thoughtfully. Is it necessary? Does it help you or others in your firm? Such analysis can lead to constructive talks with your manager. He may be able to eliminate those items that serve little or no purpose, or he may get the home office to take care of them.

MAKE GREATER USE OF THE TELEPHONE

Skilled telephone salesmen will tell you that they can sell as much of certain products and services by telephone as face-to-face salesmen can. And they can show figures to substantiate such claims.

All face-to-face salesmen must use the telephone at times. Yet many of them shy away from using it to full advantage. They need to develop a feeling for this instrument, such as the telephone salesmen have. What is needed is practice (see Chapter 12).

MAKE FULL USE OF YOUR SELLING HOURS

On the hundreds of observation trips I have made with salesmen in many lines I have often found men who habitually start late, quit early, or both. Sometimes they will rationalize: "You can't call as early as nine o'clock," or "There's no use making a call after four in the afternoon."

Everybody likes to squeeze in a little more personal time on occasion. But those who make full use of their selling hours on most days usually bring in more business, earn more, and command the respect of their customers and prospects.

One salesman who works out of Los Angeles makes a practice of calling upon selected prospective distributors after five o'clock. Not only does he bring in more distributors for this billion-dollar corporation, but the quality of his accounts is unusually good.

"One of these distributors," he says, "specifically told me that he signed because he believed that a man who was willing to work overtime on prospective accounts was the sincere and dedicated type of salesman he wanted to call on him. There are times when I knock off before five, but I find that going after important accounts regardless of time really pays off."

BUILDING THE HABIT

There's no time like now to start managing your time more effectively. Building the habit of spending your time where it counts the most begins when you work out a cream-separating plan geared to your circumstances.

To add more selling time to your working day, prepare a time budget first. Then build your workday activities around a first-things-first time control plan, in the manner of Ivy Lee's $25,000 idea. Beyond that, just two things are necessary:

1. The 25 points outlined above comprise the basic framework of any habit-building plan. Consider those points that you believe you can apply to best advantage. Then concentrate on each one in turn until it becomes a habit.

2. Add any other time-managing plan you feel may be valuable in your circumstances. Many salesmen have picked

up other ways of improving time management. From your own experience, and by exchanging ideas with your fellow salesmen, you can surely add some useful methods of your own.

You have the basic habit-building ingredients. What remains is to apply them. Start now—and you'll be well on your way to more effective time management.

15

Following Through

You have just completed the program embodied in *There IS a Better Way to Sell,* with the exception of the most important phase: follow-through.

If you have adopted the approach suggested in the text, you have considered, one at a time, seven ways to improve your productivity. After each, you developed a habit-building plan to fit your particular needs. And if you have kept at it, you now know from experience that the plan works.

Your Self-Development Program

Fortunately, improvement can continue without end, provided only that you do a good job of following through. A checklist can be of considerable help. That's why the seven ways to improve sales year after year are given on the reverse side of the O PIB'ROC pocket card that comes with this book. In case the card is not handy, the copy follows:

Manage by objectives: Develop your own bold objectives and "live" them on a daily basis—the most effective of all motivating forces.

Apply principles of communication and selling: Acquire essential habits one at a time. (The front side of the card lists these principles. For details, see the end of Chapter 9: "Closing.")

Sell more creatively: Find his problem, help solve it. Exchange creative selling experiences with others.

Use selling tools: Make better and increasing use of visual aids, demonstrations, promotions, telephone.

Improve recurring presentations: Thoroughly review your approaches—one at a time.

Manage your time: Proportion effort to potential. Preplan each year, each month, each day.

Sell yourself: Gain added rapport by thoughtfully adopting ways and means best suited to *your* personality.

The first way to improve your sales is to apply the management-by-objectives approach to your territory. Each year, or each quarter, you can lift your sights in the light of added experience. You can then revise your objectives so they are more in keeping with your increasing capacity. And when you live those objectives on a daily basis, you have the most effective of all motivating forces—the pull of your own aims. This is perhaps the most important follow-through step, the one that will yield the biggest returns both in sales and in your personal life.

When you set specific figure goals for your territory, and when you thoughtfully fuse the plans of action you outlined at the end of each chapter, you have an excellent self-development program—one which positively assures you of continuing growth.

DON'T BITE OFF MORE THAN YOU CAN CHEW

Following through requires review. But don't do everything in one big burst. It won't work.

If, however, you have followed the plan in the text, you know that it does work when you concentrate on one or a few things at a time rather than a lot.

For your review, select first the phase where you think you will gain most—for instance, more creative selling or a specific recurring situation which needs strengthening. Develop specific objectives for what you would like to accomplish in this area. Then focus on that topic for as long as you need to achieve those objectives.

Plan to review the entire book in this manner every year or every two years, thus developing continuing improvement in each phase.

For improvement in managing your time and selling yourself, the key is to strengthen your habits in these areas. Review the text, concentrate on one of these topics. Exchange experiences with fellow salesmen, and you will surely get worthwhile ideas for improvement.

Most important, plan to strengthen those habits that will improve your communication and selling skills. You do not need to let any day go by in which you fail to give consideration to the application of these basic principles. Review them consciously before and after making your sales calls. Make use of them also when you are planning purposeful communication for your activities in organizations, in business, civic, or social affairs, or in your home life. Make frequent use of the O PIB'ROC pocket card.

Give ample attention to the principle of preparation. It's the key to ever increasing knowledge of your products, your markets, your customers and prospects, your competitors' offerings. You'll get best results by adopting a definite plan for learning—and a timetable.

THE ROAD AHEAD

If you develop specific and bold sales objectives for six months or a year ahead and follow through each day to the best of your ability, you will discover that this technique is a truly valuable way to help you increase your productivity.

You can make additional significant gains by applying these management-by-objectives techniques to the years ahead. How will you be doing 5, 10, or 15 years from now? Will you plan to be a top man in your organization? Will your earnings double within the next five years—an expectation which Dick Gleason, a well-known and able career counselor in Chicago, states is a practical objective for most men on the move?

Or perhaps your long-range objective is sales management. You look forward to helping other salesmen to motivate themselves to higher achievement, apply basic principles of communication and selling consciously and more consistently, improve in product knowledge and application, and sell more creatively—in short, to apply the fundamentals of selling more intensively and effectively.

In that event, you can seek and find more ways of applying management practices in your current job. You can do more to help fellow salesmen or distributors' salesmen to be more effective. You can develop selling tools which you and others in your organization can use to advantage.

You can read books and articles, take courses pertaining to management practices, and plan to meet with salesmen and sales managers to exchange ideas on means of stimulating and achieving continued sales improvement.

When you know clearly and objectively what you want to be doing in the years ahead, you act accordingly. "If you only care enough for a result," said Ralph Waldo Emerson, "you almost certainly attain it. If you wish to be rich, you will be rich; if you wish to be learned, you will be learned; if you wish to be good, you will be good. Only you must, then, really wish these things and wish them exclusively, and not wish at the same time a hundred other incompatible things just as strongly."

Whatever your aim in the field of selling, you have a sound and continuing guide in *There IS a Better Way to Sell*.